A Beginner's Journey into HVAC

Mastering the Basics of Heating, Ventilation, and Cooling Systems

Daniel B. Simmons

Dedication

To my family, whose unwavering support and encouragement have fueled my passion for sharing knowledge.

To my mentors and colleagues in the HVAC industry, who have guided me with their wisdom and experience.

And to every beginner taking their first steps into the world of heating, ventilation, and air conditioning may this book be your trusted guide on your journey to understanding and mastering the essentials of HVAC.

Daniel B. Simmons

Table of Contents

Introduction

Welcome to "HVAC for Beginners: The Ultimate Guide to Heating, Ventilation, and Air Conditioning Systems." If you've ever wondered how your home stays warm in the winter, cool in the summer, or how fresh air circulates through a building, you are in the right place. HVAC systems play a vital role in our daily lives, and understanding how they work can make a big difference in how we manage comfort, energy efficiency, and health in our homes and workplaces. This book is your gateway to learning all about HVAC in a simple, easy-to-follow way, even if you have no prior experience.

What is HVAC

HVAC stands for Heating, Ventilation, and Air Conditioning. It refers to the systems and technologies that provide heating, cooling, and fresh air in buildings. These systems are designed to regulate indoor temperature, improve air quality, and maintain a comfortable environment for people.

Let us break it down:

a. Heating: This part of HVAC is all about keeping you warm when it is cold outside. It includes systems like furnaces, boilers, and heat pumps that generate and distribute heat to maintain a comfortable indoor temperature.

b. Ventilation: Ventilation ensures that fresh air circulates inside a building and removes stale air, odors, and pollutants. It can be natural, like opening windows, or mechanical, using fans and ducts to move air around.

c. Air Conditioning: Air conditioning cools your indoor spaces during hot weather. It removes heat and humidity from the air, making your environment more comfortable.

Together, these three components work to create a living or working space that feels just right not too hot, not too cold, and with clean, breathable air.

Whether you live in a small apartment, a house, or work in a large office building, chances are an HVAC system is quietly working behind the scenes to keep you comfortable.

Why HVAC Matters: Comfort, Health, and Energy Efficiency

HVAC systems do more than just control temperature. They play a critical role in several aspects of our daily lives, including comfort, health, and energy efficiency. Let us take a closer look at why HVAC matters:

a. Comfort: Have you ever stepped into a cozy, warm house after being out in the freezing cold. Or felt the refreshing cool air of air conditioning on a hot summer day? That's the magic of HVAC systems. They ensure that indoor environments stay comfortable no matter the weather outside. Modern HVAC systems can even be tailored to individual preferences, allowing you to set the perfect temperature for every room.

b. Health: Indoor air quality has a direct impact on our health. Poor ventilation can lead to a buildup of dust, allergens, mold, and even harmful pollutants. This can cause respiratory problems, allergies, and other health issues. A good HVAC system helps keep the air clean and fresh by filtering out contaminants and providing proper ventilation. Some advanced systems even include air purifiers that kill bacteria and viruses, creating a healthier environment for everyone inside.

c. Energy Efficiency: Energy efficiency is an increasingly important consideration in today's world. A well-designed HVAC system not only keeps you comfortable but also uses energy efficiently, reducing your utility bills and lowering your carbon footprint. Modern HVAC technologies, such as programmable thermostats and high-efficiency systems, make it possible to stay comfortable while conserving energy. This is good for the environment and for your wallet.

 HVAC systems are much more than just a luxury. They are essential for maintaining comfort, protecting our health, and promoting energy efficiency. As you explore this book, you will gain a deeper understanding of how these systems work and how they can be optimized for your specific needs. Whether you are a homeowner, a curious learner, or someone looking to start a career in the HVAC industry, this guide is here to help you take the first steps into the fascinating world of heating, ventilation, and air conditioning.

Overview of the Book: How to Use This Guide

This book is designed to be your go-to resource for learning about HVAC systems, no matter your level of experience. To make it as helpful and easy to navigate as possible, here is how you can use this guide:

a. Step-by-Step Learning: Each chapter builds on the previous one, starting with the basics and moving toward more advanced topics. If you are new to HVAC, it is best to read the book in order.

b. Comprehensive Coverage: We have divided the book into sections that cover heating, ventilation, air conditioning, installation, maintenance, and more. You can jump to specific sections if you are looking for information on a particular topic.

c. Simple Explanations: HVAC concepts are explained in plain, natural English without unnecessary jargon. Technical terms are clearly defined in the glossary for quick reference.

d. Practical Tips: You will find helpful tips and actionable advice throughout the book. Whether you are a homeowner looking to improve your HVAC system or someone considering a career in the industry, this book offers valuable insights.

e. Resources and Checklists: At the end of the book, you'll find resources, maintenance checklists, and other tools to help you apply what you have learned.

By the time you finish this book, you will have a solid foundation in HVAC systems and the confidence to take the next step, whether it is maintaining your own system, making energy-efficient upgrades, or pursuing a career in the field.

A Brief History of HVAC Systems

The concept of heating and cooling indoor spaces has been around for centuries, though HVAC technology as we know it today is relatively modern. Here is a brief look at the history of HVAC systems:

a. Early Heating Systems: The earliest forms of heating date back to ancient civilizations. For example; The Romans used hypocaust systems, where hot air from a furnace was channeled under floors and through walls to warm their buildings. In medieval Europe, fireplaces became the primary source of heat in homes and castles. These early methods were inefficient and required constant attention, but they laid the groundwork for modern heating technologies.

b. The Birth of Modern Heating: In the 19th century, significant advancements were made; the invention of the cast-iron radiator and steam heating systems revolutionized how homes and buildings were heated. Central heating systems, using boilers and radiators, became more common in the late 1800s.

c. Ventilation Milestones: Ventilation became a focus during the Industrial Revolution, as factories and urban areas experienced poor air quality. Advances included; Mechanical ventilation systems, such as fans and ductwork, were developed to improve airflow in buildings. By the early 20th century, air filters were introduced to remove dust and pollutants from indoor air.

d. The Rise of Air Conditioning; Air conditioning as we know it began in the early 1900s: In 1902, Willis Carrier designed the first modern air conditioning system to control temperature and humidity in a printing plant. By the 1920s, air conditioning was introduced in theaters and large buildings, and by the 1950s, it became more common in homes.

e. Modern HVAC Systems: In Today's technology, HVAC systems are more advanced than ever. They use energy-efficient technologies, smart thermostats, and even renewable energy sources like solar power. Innovations continue to make HVAC systems more effective, environmentally friendly, and tailored to individual needs. Understanding this history helps us appreciate how far HVAC systems have come and how they have shaped the way we live and work.

Part 1: HVAC Fundamentals

Chapter One: The Basics of Heating, Ventilation, and Air Conditioning

HVAC systems are designed to control three key aspects of indoor environments: heating, ventilation, and air conditioning. Here is an overview of what these systems do:

a. Heating: This function ensures that indoor spaces stay warm during cold weather. Heating systems, such as furnaces or boilers, generate heat and distribute it throughout the building using ducts, radiators, or other methods.

b. Ventilation: Ventilation is about moving air in and out of a building. It helps to bring in fresh outdoor air and remove indoor air that might be stale or contaminated. Proper ventilation improves air quality and ensures a healthy environment.

c. Air Conditioning: Air conditioning keeps spaces cool during hot weather. It works by removing heat and humidity from the indoor air, creating a more comfortable and pleasant atmosphere.

Each part of an HVAC system works together to create an indoor environment that is comfortable, clean, and efficient. These systems are found in homes, offices, factories, and many other types of buildings, making them an essential part of modern life.

1.1 Understanding Thermal Comfort

Thermal comfort is the state of mind where a person feels satisfied with the temperature and conditions of their indoor environment. Achieving thermal comfort is one of the primary goals of HVAC systems, and it involves more than just regulating temperature. Let us explore the key factors that influence thermal comfort and how HVAC systems help maintain it.

a. Temperature Regulation: Temperature is the most critical factor in thermal comfort. People generally feel comfortable within a specific temperature range, often between 68°F and 74°F (20°C to 23°C). HVAC systems are designed to maintain this range by heating during cold weather and cooling during hot weather. Thermostats and programmable controls allow precise adjustments to suit individual preferences.

b. Humidity Levels: Humidity plays a significant role in how we perceive temperature. High humidity makes the air feel warmer than it actually is because it slows down the evaporation of sweat from our skin. Low humidity, on the other hand, can make the air feel colder and may cause dryness in the skin and respiratory system. Ideal indoor humidity levels range between 30% and 50%. Modern HVAC systems often include humidifiers or dehumidifiers to maintain these levels.

c. Air Movement and Circulation: Proper air movement helps distribute heat and cool air evenly throughout a space, preventing hot or cold spots. It also enhances the evaporation of moisture from the skin, improving comfort. Ceiling fans, vents, and ductwork all contribute to effective air circulation. HVAC systems are designed to optimize air movement, ensuring every corner of a room feels comfortable.

d. Building Design and Insulation: The design and insulation of a building greatly affect thermal comfort. Well-insulated walls, windows, and roofs help maintain indoor temperatures by reducing heat loss in winter and heat gain in summer. HVAC systems work more efficiently in well-insulated buildings, as less energy is required to maintain desired temperature levels.

e. Personal Factors: Thermal comfort is subjective and varies from person to person. Factors such as age, activity level, clothing, and overall health influence how individuals perceive temperature. For example, someone engaged in physical activity may feel warm even in a cooler room, while someone sitting still might feel cold. HVAC systems with zoning capabilities allow different areas of a building to be set at different temperatures, catering to individual needs.

f. External Weather Conditions: Outdoor weather impacts indoor thermal comfort. On a hot summer day, the sun's heat can make indoor spaces uncomfortably warm, while cold winter winds can cause drafts. HVAC systems counteract these effects by adjusting indoor conditions to create a consistent and comfortable environment.

g. The Importance of Thermal Comfort: Achieving thermal comfort is not just about feeling good; it also affects productivity, health, and well-being. Comfortable indoor environments help people concentrate better, sleep more soundly, and enjoy their living and working spaces. Poor thermal comfort, on the other hand, can lead to discomfort, reduced productivity, and even health issues such as dehydration or respiratory problems. By understanding the factors that influence thermal comfort, HVAC systems can be designed and maintained to provide optimal conditions for any space. This ensures that people remain comfortable, healthy, and satisfied in their indoor environments.

1.2 The Role of Air Movement and Humidity

Air movement and humidity are two crucial factors that significantly impact indoor comfort and air quality. Together, they play a vital role in creating a balanced and healthy environment. Let us break down their importance and how HVAC systems help manage them effectively.

A. Air Movement: Air movement refers to how air flows through a space. Proper air circulation is essential for distributing heat, cooling, and fresh air evenly throughout a room or building. Here is why it matters:

i. Temperature Distribution: Without adequate air movement, some areas in a space may feel too hot or too cold. For example, in winter, warm air from heating systems can rise to the ceiling, leaving the lower areas cooler. Fans, vents, and ductwork ensure that air is circulated evenly, eliminating uncomfortable hot or cold spots.

ii. Fresh Air Supply: Air movement helps bring fresh outdoor air into a building while removing stale indoor air. This exchange improves air quality and prevents the buildup of odors, pollutants, and carbon dioxide.

iii. Comfort and Skin Cooling: Air movement enhances the evaporation of sweat from the skin, making people feel cooler and more comfortable, especially in warm conditions. Even a gentle breeze from a fan can make a significant difference.

iv. Prevention of Moisture Buildup: Proper air circulation prevents moisture from accumulating on surfaces, reducing the risk of mold and mildew growth.

How HVAC Systems Control Air Movement

HVAC systems are designed to optimize air movement using:

i. Ductwork and Vents: These distribute heated or cooled air throughout a building.

ii. Fans: Ceiling fans exhaust fans, and inline fans help circulate air and maintain a steady flow.

iii. Air Balancing: Professional HVAC technicians ensure that air is distributed evenly across all areas by adjusting ducts and vents.

B. Humidity: Humidity refers to the amount of moisture in the air. It has a significant impact on comfort, health, and even the structural integrity of a building. Maintaining the right humidity level is a critical function of HVAC systems. Here is why:

i. Comfort: High humidity makes the air feel warmer, while low humidity can make it feel cooler. For example, in summer, high humidity can make a room feel stuffy and uncomfortable. In winter, low humidity can cause dry skin, chapped lips, and static electricity.

ii. Health: Excessive humidity promotes the growth of mold, dust mites, and bacteria, which can trigger allergies and respiratory problems. On the other hand, very low humidity can dry out the mucous membranes in the nose and throat, making people more susceptible to colds and infections.

iii. Protection of Belongings: High humidity can damage furniture, electronics, and wooden structures by causing warping or rust. Low humidity can cause wooden items to crack or split.

How HVAC Systems Manage Humidity

Modern HVAC systems include features to control indoor humidity:

i. Dehumidifiers: These devices remove excess moisture from the air, making the environment more comfortable and preventing issues like mold growth.

ii. Humidifiers: In dry conditions, humidifiers add moisture to the air to prevent dryness and discomfort.

iii. Air Conditioners: Most air conditioning systems naturally dehumidify the air as they cool it, helping to maintain balanced humidity levels.

iv. Ventilation Systems: Proper ventilation ensures that moisture-laden air is expelled and replaced with drier, fresh air.

Ideal Humidity Levels: The recommended indoor humidity level is between 30% and 50%. Staying within this range ensures optimal comfort, health, and protection for your belongings.

Balancing Air Movement and Humidity

Achieving the right balance of air movement and humidity is essential for creating a comfortable and healthy indoor environment. HVAC systems are designed to work seamlessly to regulate these factors, providing consistent comfort year-round. By understanding

Chapter Two: Key Components of HVAC Systems

HVAC systems are designed to control the temperature, airflow, and air quality inside buildings. While furnaces, boilers, heat pumps, air conditioners, ventilation ducts, and thermostats are key parts of the system,

2.1 Furnaces and Boilers in HVAC Systems

Furnaces and boilers are both essential heating components of HVAC (Heating, Ventilation, and Air Conditioning) systems. They are designed to provide warmth to homes or buildings, especially during cold weather. While they both serve the same purpose of heating, they do so in different ways.

a. Furnaces

A furnace is a device that heats the air in your home. It works by burning fuel (such as natural gas, propane, or oil) or using electricity to generate heat. Once the air is heated, a blower fan pushes it through a system of ducts and into different rooms of the building. This distribution of warm air keeps the space comfortable during winter.

Here is how a furnace works:
i. Heating: When the thermostat senses that the temperature in the room is too low, it sends a signal to the furnace to turn on. The furnace heats up the air.
Circulation: The heated air is then pushed through ducts by a fan, and it enters the rooms of the house via vents.
ii. Exhaust: After the furnace burns fuel, it produces gases as a byproduct. These gases are vented out of the home through a flue or chimney.
iii. Furnaces are commonly used because they are fast at heating and can easily heat an entire home or building. They are most often used in colder climates where consistent, reliable heat is needed.

b. Boilers

Boilers, unlike furnaces, heat water or produce steam to distribute heat. Instead of blowing warm air, boilers use hot water or steam to heat the building. The heated water travels through pipes to radiators or baseboard heaters placed in different rooms. In some systems, heated water can also be used for under floor heating.

Here is how a boiler works:

i. Heating: The boiler heats water using fuel, which could be natural gas, oil, or electricity. The water inside the boiler is heated to a high temperature and turns into steam or stays as hot water.

ii. Circulation: The steam or hot water travels through pipes to radiators or under floor heating systems throughout the building.

iii. Distribution: As the steam or hot water moves through the radiators, it releases heat, warming the air around it. The cooled water or steam returns to the boiler to be reheated again.

Boilers are ideal for homes that have radiators or in-floor heating systems. They are also a good choice in areas where forced-air heating (like furnaces) is less common. One of the advantages of boilers is that they can provide a more even heat because they do not rely on air movement, which can dry out the air.

Differences between Furnaces and Boilers

i. Method of Heating: Furnaces heat air and circulate it through ducts, while boilers heat water or produce steam and distribute heat through pipes.

ii. Comfort Level: Boilers can provide a more even and gentle heat, whereas furnaces can sometimes create hot and cold spots in rooms.

iii. Air Quality: Furnaces can stir up dust and allergens because they circulate air, but boilers do not move air, which can help maintain better air quality.

iv. Energy Efficiency: Boilers can be more energy-efficient because they do not lose heat through ducts, whereas furnaces can lose heat in the ducts if they are not well-insulated.

Choosing Between a Furnace and a Boiler

When deciding between a furnace and a boiler, consider factors like the size of your home, your climate, and your heating preferences. Furnaces are generally less expensive to install and provide heat quickly, making them a good choice for colder climates. Boilers, on the other hand, can offer a more consistent heat and are ideal for homes with radiators or radiant floor heating systems.

In conclusion, both furnaces and boilers are crucial heating components in an HVAC system, and choosing the right one depends on your specific needs, home layout, and climate conditions.

2.2 Heat Pumps in HVAC Systems

A heat pump is an important component of HVAC systems that provides both heating and cooling. It is a versatile and energy-efficient option, especially in regions with moderate climates. The primary function of a heat pump is to move heat from one place to another, either bringing heat into a building to warm it up in winter or removing heat from the building to cool it in summer.

How a Heat Pump Works

A heat pump works like a refrigerator, but instead of keeping things cool, it either heats or cools the air inside your home. It does this by using a special fluid called refrigerant, which can absorb and release heat as it moves through the system.

i. Heating Mode: During colder months, the heat pump extracts heat from the outside air (even when it is cold outside) and transfers it inside to warm the building. The refrigerant absorbs heat from the outdoor air, and then it is compressed to a higher temperature and sent inside. A fan blows the heated air into your home to raise the temperature.

ii. Cooling Mode: In warmer months, the process is reversed. The heat pump absorbs heat from inside the house and releases it outside. It works like an air conditioner by circulating the refrigerant through a coil, absorbing the heat from the indoor air, and expelling it outdoors.

Parts of a Heat Pump

A heat pump consists of several parts that work together:

i. Evaporator Coil: This is the part that absorbs heat from the air (when in heating mode) or releases heat (when in cooling mode).

ii. Condenser Coil: This is where the heat is either released or absorbed, depending on the mode.

iii. Compressor: The compressor pressurizes the refrigerant, which helps it absorb or release heat more effectively.

iv. Expansion Valve: This controls the flow of refrigerant to maintain proper pressure and temperature in the system.

Advantages of Heat Pumps

i. Energy Efficiency: Heat pumps are energy-efficient because they do not generate heat. Instead, they move it from one place to another, which uses less energy than traditional heating systems. This can result in lower utility bills.

ii. Dual Function: One of the biggest benefits of a heat pump is that it provides both heating and cooling in one system, which makes it a versatile choice for year-round comfort.

iii. Environmentally Friendly: Since heat pumps use electricity rather than fossil fuels (like gas or oil); they are generally better for the environment and produce fewer carbon emissions.

iv. Consistent Comfort: Heat pumps provide a steady and consistent temperature in the home, without the hot or cold bursts that some traditional heating and cooling systems can create.

Limitations of Heat Pumps

i. Less Effective in Extreme Cold: Heat pumps work best in mild to moderate climates. In extremely cold temperatures, they may struggle to extract enough heat from the outside air to effectively heat the home. In such conditions, a backup heating system may be needed.

ii. Initial Cost: While heat pumps can save money on energy bills over time, they may have a higher upfront installation cost compared to traditional heating and cooling systems.

Heat pumps are a highly efficient and environmentally friendly choice for heating and cooling a home. By transferring heat instead of generating it, heat pumps can provide consistent comfort year-round. They are a great option for moderate climates but may not be as effective in very cold areas. If you are looking for an energy-efficient way to maintain a comfortable indoor environment, a heat pump is a solid option to consider in your HVAC system.

2.3 Air Conditioners in HVAC Systems

An air conditioner (AC) is a crucial component of HVAC systems, designed to cool the air inside buildings, especially during hot weather. It helps create a comfortable environment by lowering the temperature and reducing humidity levels. Air conditioners are commonly used in homes, offices, and other buildings to keep indoor spaces cool and pleasant.

How Air Conditioners Work

Air conditioners work by removing heat from the indoor air and transferring it outside. Here is a step-by-step explanation of how they work:

i. Absorbing Heat: The air conditioner has an evaporator coil inside the unit. A fan blows warm indoor air over this coil. The evaporator coil contains refrigerant, a special fluid that absorbs heat from the air.

ii. Cooling the Air: As the refrigerant absorbs heat, it turns from a cold liquid into a warm gas. This process cools the air, and the fan blows the cooled air back into the room.

iii. Releasing Heat: The warm refrigerant gas is then sent to the compressor unit, typically located outside the building. The compressor pressurizes the refrigerant, turning it into a hot, high-pressure gas.

iv. Expelling Heat: The hot refrigerant gas is then passed through the condenser coils, which are also located outside the building. Here, the heat is released into the outdoor air, and the refrigerant cools down and turns back into a liquid.

v. Cycle Repeats: The refrigerant returns to the evaporator coil inside the air conditioner, and the process repeats. The air conditioner continues to absorb heat from the indoor air, cool it, and release the heat outside.

Key Components of an Air Conditioner

i. Evaporator Coil: Located inside the unit, this coil absorbs heat from the air. It is essential for cooling the indoor air.

ii. Compressor: Found outside the building, the compressor pressurizes the refrigerant, helping it to release heat outdoors.

iii. Condenser Coil: This coil, also located outside, releases the heat from the refrigerant into the outside air.

iv. Expansion Valve: This controls the flow of refrigerant into the evaporator coil and helps maintain the right pressure and temperature in the system.

v. Fan: The fan blows warm air over the evaporator coil to be cooled, and then it circulates the cool air back into the room.

Energy Efficiency and Maintenance

Air conditioners can be energy-hungry appliances, but newer models are designed to be more energy-efficient. Look for units with a higher SEER (Seasonal Energy Efficiency Ratio) rating, which indicates better energy performance.

Regular maintenance is also important for keeping your air conditioner running efficiently. This includes:

a. Changing or cleaning filters: Dirty filters can reduce airflow and make the system work harder.

b. Checking refrigerant levels: Low refrigerant levels can affect the cooling performance.

c. Cleaning the condenser coils: Dirt and debris can block the coils, reducing their ability to expel heat.

d. Inspecting the thermostat: A malfunctioning thermostat can prevent the system from cooling properly.

Air conditioners are a key part of HVAC systems, providing cooling and comfort during hot weather. By removing heat and moisture from the air, they help keep indoor spaces comfortable and healthy. Whether you're using a window unit or a central air system, air conditioners are essential for maintaining a cool and pleasant environment in your home or office. Regular maintenance and energy-efficient models can ensure that your air conditioner continues to perform at its best.

2.4 Ventilation Ducts in HVAC Systems

Ventilation ducts are an important part of an HVAC (Heating, Ventilation, and Air Conditioning) system. They are responsible for distributing the heated or cooled air throughout a building, ensuring that every room or space is comfortable and has good air quality. Without ventilation ducts, it would be difficult for air to flow efficiently and evenly through the system.

What Are Ventilation Ducts

Ventilation ducts are networks of tubes or channels that carry air to different parts of a building. These ducts are typically made of materials like sheet metal, fiberglass, or flexible plastic. The air that flows through these ducts can either be heated or cooled, depending on the HVAC system settings.

There are two main types of ducts:

i. Supply Ducts: These ducts carry heated or cooled air from the HVAC system to the rooms in a building. The supply ducts connect to vents or registers in each room, where the air is released.

ii. Return Ducts: These ducts carry air back from the rooms to the HVAC system, where it can be filtered and re-conditioned before being circulated again.

How Do Ventilation Ducts Work

The main purpose of ventilation ducts is to move air throughout the building. Here is how they work in a typical HVAC system:

i. Air Intake: The HVAC system draws in air from the rooms through the return ducts. This air can be filtered to remove dust, dirt, and allergens before being heated or cooled.

ii. Air Conditioning or Heating: The system either cools the air (through an air conditioner) or heats it (through a furnace or heat pump).

iii. Air Distribution: The treated air is then pushed through the supply ducts by a fan or blower. The air is delivered through vents or registers into the rooms to maintain the desired temperature.

iv. Return to the System: After circulating through the building, the air returns to the system via the return ducts, where it is filtered again, and the process starts over.

Importance of Ventilation Ducts

i. Efficient Airflow: Ventilation ducts are crucial for ensuring that air flows efficiently throughout the building. Proper airflow helps maintain a consistent temperature in every room, preventing hot or cold spots.

ii. Air Quality: Ducts also help improve indoor air quality by circulating fresh, filtered air. They help remove dust, allergens, and other pollutants from the indoor environment, making it healthier to breathe.

iii. Comfort: Well-designed ductwork allows for even temperature distribution, which means that each room in a house or building can stay at a comfortable temperature. Without ducts, rooms would become stuffy or excessively hot or cold.

iv. Energy Efficiency: When ducts are properly installed and sealed, they help the HVAC system work more efficiently, reducing energy consumption and lowering utility bills.

Materials Used for Ventilation Ducts

Ventilation ducts can be made from several different materials, each with its advantages:

i. Sheet Metal Ducts: These are the most common type of ducts, often made from galvanized steel. They are strong, durable, and provide good airflow. However, they can be heavy and expensive to install.

ii. Flexible Ducts: Made from a flexible material, these ducts are easy to install and can be bent to fit in tight spaces. They are often used in homes with limited space for traditional ductwork. However, they may not be as durable as metal ducts and can reduce airflow over time if damaged.

iii. Fiberglass Ducts: These ducts are made of fiberglass and are known for their insulation properties. They help maintain the temperature of the air as it travels through the system and reduce energy loss.

iv. Fabric Ducts: Made from durable fabric, these ducts are used in some commercial settings. They are lightweight, flexible, and easy to install but may not be suitable for every type of HVAC system.

Common Issues with Ventilation Ducts

While ventilation ducts are essential for the proper functioning of an HVAC system, they can experience some problems:

i. Leaks: Ducts can develop leaks over time, especially at the joints. These leaks reduce airflow, because energy loss and can lead to higher utility bills.

ii. Blockages: Dust, dirt, and debris can build up inside ducts, blocking the flow of air. This can reduce the system's efficiency and lead to poor air quality.

iii. Poor Insulation: If ducts are poorly insulated, they can lose heat or cool air as it travels through the system. This results in energy loss and makes the HVAC system work harder to maintain the desired temperature.

iv. Improper Sizing: Ducts that is too small or too large for the HVAC system can cause airflow problems. Small ducts can restrict air, while large ducts can result in uneven air distribution.

Maintaining Ventilation Ducts

To keep ventilation ducts in good condition and ensure efficient airflow, regular maintenance is important:

i. Cleaning: Ducts should be cleaned regularly to remove dust, dirt, and allergens. A professional can use special tools to clean the ducts and ensure the air quality remains good.

ii. Inspection: Periodically checking the ducts for leaks, damage, or blockages helps identify problems early, before they affect the system's performance.

iii. Sealing: If leaks are found, they should be sealed to prevent air from escaping and to maintain the efficiency of the HVAC system.

Ventilation ducts are a key part of any HVAC system. They allow air to be distributed evenly throughout a building, ensuring comfort and good air quality. Properly designed, installed and maintained ducts are essential for making the HVAC system work efficiently, saving energy, and improving indoor air quality. Regular maintenance can help prevent issues like leaks, blockages, and poor airflow, ensuring that your home or building stays comfortable year-round.

2.5 Thermostats

A thermostat is a key component of any HVAC (Heating, Ventilation, and Air Conditioning) system. It acts as the control center for regulating the temperature in a building, ensuring that the indoor environment remains comfortable. Whether you're heating your home in the winter or cooling it in the summer, the thermostat is responsible for maintaining the temperature you set.

What Is a Thermostat

A thermostat is a device that monitors the current temperature of a room or building and controls the HVAC system to keep the temperature at your desired level. It acts as a bridge between you and your heating or cooling system. When the temperature falls below or rises above the set point, the thermostat signals the HVAC system to either turn on or off, making adjustments as needed.

How Does a Thermostat Work

Thermostats operate by sensing the temperature in a room using a sensor, typically inside the thermostat itself. Here is a simple explanation of how it works:

i. Temperature Detection: The thermostat continuously monitors the temperature in the room.

ii. Comparison to Desired Temperature: When the room temperature is different from the set temperature (the temperature you want to maintain), the thermostat compares the two.

iii. Turning the HVAC System On/Off: If the room is too cold and the temperature is lower than the set temperature, the thermostat signals the heating system (like a furnace or heat pump) to turn on and start warming the air. If the room is too hot and the temperature is higher than the set temperature, the thermostat signals the cooling system (like an air conditioner) to turn on and start cooling the air.

iv. Maintaining the Set Temperature: The thermostat continues to monitor the temperature and adjusts the heating or cooling as needed to keep the room at the desired temperature.

Types of Thermostats

There are several types of thermostats available, each with different features. Here are the main types:

a. Manual Thermostats: These are simple, mechanical devices where you manually adjust the temperature using a dial or slider. You have to set the temperature each time you need it, and they don't have any advanced features like programming or remote control.

b. Programmable Thermostats: These thermostats allow you to set a schedule for your heating and cooling. You can program them to automatically adjust the temperature at different times of the day. For example, you might set the temperature to lower while you're at work and raise it before you come home. This can help save energy and improve comfort.

c. Smart Thermostats: These are the most advanced type of thermostat. Smart thermostats can be controlled remotely via a Smartphone, tablet, or computer. They often learn your habits over time and can adjust the temperature based on your schedule and preferences. Some smart thermostats can even detect when you're home or away and adjust the temperature accordingly to save energy. They can be integrated with other smart home devices for even more convenience.

Advantages of Thermostats

i. Energy Efficiency: Thermostats help save energy by ensuring that your HVAC system only operates when necessary. A well-programmed thermostat can reduce heating and cooling when you're not home or during the night when you do not need it as much.

ii. Comfort: A thermostat maintains a consistent temperature, so you do not have to worry about the temperature fluctuating too much. This ensures that your home or building stays comfortable year-round.

iii. Convenience: Programmable and smart thermostats allow for more flexibility, letting you adjust the temperature according to your schedule or control it remotely. This makes it easier to maintain comfort without constantly making manual adjustments.

iv. Cost Savings: By efficiently controlling the temperature and reducing energy consumption, thermostats can help lower your heating and cooling bills.

Common Features of Modern Thermostats

i. Touch screen Displays: Many modern thermostats come with a touch screen display that's easy to read and adjust.

ii. Wi-Fi Connectivity: Some thermostats can connect to your home's Wi-Fi network, allowing you to control them remotely via an app or through voice commands with virtual assistants like Google Assistant.

iii. Learning Features: Smart thermostats can learn your heating and cooling patterns and automatically adjust based on your habits. For example, if you tend to adjust the temperature at certain times of day, the thermostat will remember and do it for you.

iv. Geo-fencing: Some smart thermostats have geo-fencing technology, which means they can detect when you are leaving or coming home based on the location of your Smartphone. This allows the thermostat to adjust the temperature automatically for energy savings when you are away.

Common Issues with Thermostats

While thermostats are generally reliable, they can sometimes experience problems:

i. Battery Failure: Some thermostats run on batteries, which can wear out over time and cause the thermostat to stop working. It's important to change the batteries regularly if needed.

ii. Calibration Problems: If the thermostat is not reading the temperature correctly, it might cause the HVAC system to turn on or off at the wrong times. This can result in discomfort or energy waste.

iii. Wiring Issues: If the thermostat is wired incorrectly, it may not be able to communicate with the HVAC system properly, causing malfunctioning or failure to control the system.

Maintaining Your Thermostat

To ensure your thermostat continues to work properly:

i. Change the batteries regularly (for battery-operated models).

ii. Check for dust or debris that might be blocking the sensors or display, especially in older models.

iii. Calibrate your thermostat if you notice any temperature discrepancies.

iv. Update smart thermostats to the latest software to ensure the system works efficiently.

Thermostats are a vital part of HVAC systems, helping to control the temperature and maintain comfort in your home or building. They offer many benefits, from energy efficiency to convenience, and come in different types to suit different needs. Whether you choose a basic manual thermostat or an advanced smart model, having a thermostat ensures your HVAC system runs effectively, saving energy and keeping the indoor environment comfortable. Regular maintenance and proper use will help you get the most out of your thermostat.

Chapter 3: Common Types of HVAC Systems

Here are a few common types of HVAC systems,

3.1 Central HVAC Systems

A Central HVAC System is one of the most common types of heating, ventilation, and air conditioning systems. It is designed to heat or cool an entire building or home from one central location. These systems are typically found in larger buildings, homes, or commercial spaces where controlling the temperature and air quality in multiple rooms or areas is necessary.

How Do Central HVAC Systems Work

Central HVAC systems operate by distributing heated or cooled air through a network of ducts to various rooms in the building. The system consists of several key components that work together to regulate the indoor environment:

i. Thermostat: This device controls the temperature in the building. It senses the current temperature and signals the HVAC system to turn on or off when the desired temperature is reached.

ii. Furnace or Heat Pump: The furnace (for heating) or heat pump (for both heating and cooling) is the heart of the central HVAC system. These units heat the air (in the case of the furnace) or heat and cool the air (in the case of a heat pump) and send it through the ductwork to each room.

iii. Air Conditioner: If the system includes air conditioning, the air conditioner cools the air in the summer by removing heat from the indoor air and expelling it outside.

iv. Ductwork: Ducts are pipes or channels that carry air throughout the building. The conditioned air (heated or cooled) travels from the furnace or air conditioner through the ducts and into each room, where it is released through vents or registers.

v. Vents/Registers: These are the openings in each room where the conditioned air flows in. They are connected to the ductwork and are adjustable to control the airflow.

vi. Return Air Ducts: After the air circulates through the rooms, it returns to the HVAC system via return ducts. The air is filtered, and the process of heating or cooling starts again.

Types of Central HVAC Systems

There are different types of central HVAC systems depending on the needs of the building. Some common types include:

a. Central Heating and Air Conditioning Systems: These systems include both heating and cooling components, usually with a furnace and an air conditioner. In the winter, the furnace heats the air, and in the summer, the air conditioner cools the air.

b. Heat Pump Systems: A heat pump is a type of central HVAC system that can both heat and cool the air. In the winter, the heat pump extracts heat from the outside air and brings it inside, while in the summer, it works like an air conditioner by removing heat from the inside and releasing it outside.

c. Ductless Mini-Split Systems: Although similar to central systems, ductless systems do not require ducts. Instead, they have an outdoor unit and several small indoor units, making them ideal for homes that do not have existing ductwork. While not technically "central" in the traditional sense, they can still heat and cool multiple rooms.

Advantages of Central HVAC Systems

i. Even Temperature Distribution: Central HVAC systems provide consistent heating and cooling throughout the entire building. Because they use ducts to distribute air to every room, you can expect a uniform temperature in each area.

ii. Improved Air Quality: Central systems often include air filters that help remove dust, allergens, and pollutants from the air. This is particularly beneficial for people with allergies or respiratory issues.

iii. Convenience: These systems are easy to control, often through a central thermostat that lets you adjust the temperature for the whole house. This is more convenient than using separate units for each room.

iv. Energy Efficiency: When properly maintained, central HVAC systems can be energy-efficient. Many newer models are designed to use less energy, which can help lower your heating and cooling costs.

v. Increased Home Value: Having a central HVAC system can increase the value of your home. Many buyers look for homes with modern, efficient heating and cooling systems.

Disadvantages of Central HVAC Systems

i. Higher Installation Costs: The upfront cost of installing a central HVAC system can be high, especially if you need to install ductwork in a building that didn't previously have it.

ii. Maintenance Costs: Central HVAC systems require regular maintenance, including changing filters, cleaning ducts, and servicing the furnace or heat pump. This can add to the long-term cost of the system.

iii. Space Requirements: The system requires space for components like the furnace, air conditioner, and ductwork. This can be an issue in smaller homes where space is limited.

iv. Energy Loss: If the ductwork is not well insulated or if there are leaks, energy can be lost as the air travels through the ducts, reducing efficiency.

Maintaining a Central HVAC System

To ensure that a central HVAC system runs efficiently and lasts for many years, regular maintenance is essential. Here are some important maintenance tasks:

i. Change the air filters regularly: Dirty filters reduce airflow and can affect the efficiency of the system.

ii. Clean the ducts: Dust and debris can accumulate in the ducts, which can reduce airflow and air quality.

iii. Inspect and clean the furnace or heat pump: These components should be checked annually to ensure they are functioning properly.

iv. Check the refrigerant levels (for systems with air conditioning or heat pumps): Low refrigerant can reduce cooling efficiency.

v. Seal duct leaks: Leaks in the ductwork can cause energy loss and reduce the effectiveness of the system.

A central HVAC system is an efficient and effective way to heat and cool a large home or building. By using ducts to distribute conditioned air, it provides consistent temperature control and improves indoor air quality. While it may involve a higher initial cost for installation, the comfort, energy efficiency, and convenience it provides can make it a valuable investment for many homeowners. Regular maintenance is key to ensuring the system operates efficiently and lasts for many years.

3.2 Split Systems in HVAC

A split system is one of the most common types of HVAC (Heating, Ventilation, and Air Conditioning) systems used in homes and small commercial buildings. It is designed to provide both heating and cooling for indoor spaces in an efficient way. Unlike central systems, split systems do not rely on a large duct network to distribute air throughout the building, making them ideal for smaller spaces or homes without existing ductwork.

What Is a Split System

A split system consists of two main parts: an indoor unit and an outdoor unit. These two units are split apart, meaning that the components that heat or cool the air are housed separately. The indoor unit is responsible for the air handling and cooling or heating, while the outdoor unit performs the heavy-duty work of heating or cooling the air.

How Does a Split System Work

A split system works by using refrigerant, a chemical that can absorb and release heat, to cool or heat the air. Here is a simple explanation of how it works:

a. Cooling Mode: The outdoor unit houses the compressor, which pumps refrigerant through copper pipes to the indoor unit. The refrigerant absorbs heat from the indoor air and carries it to the outdoor unit. The indoor unit contains the evaporator coil, which cools the air as it passes over the coils. This cooled air is then blown into the room through vents or registers. The refrigerant, after absorbing the heat, is sent back to the outdoor unit, where it is cooled down and the process continues.

b. Heating Mode (For systems with a heat pump): In heating mode, the heat pump in the outdoor unit extracts heat from the outside air (even when it is cold) and transfers it indoors. The indoor unit then uses the heat absorbed by the refrigerant to warm the air and distribute it into the room.

Note: A heat pump can reverse the cooling and heating process, making it a versatile option for both heating and cooling.

Key Components of a Split System

a. Indoor Unit: The indoor unit is often called the air handler or evaporator unit. It contains the evaporator coils, a fan, and sometimes a filter to clean the air. The unit is typically mounted on a wall or in the ceiling. The fan inside the indoor unit blows the conditioned air (heated or cooled) into the room.

b. Outdoor Unit: The outdoor unit houses the compressor, which pumps refrigerant throughout the system. It also contains the condenser coil, where the refrigerant releases the heat it has absorbed from inside. This unit is typically placed outside the building, often near an exterior wall or on the roof.

c. Refrigerant Lines: Copper pipes or tubes connect the indoor and outdoor units. These lines carry refrigerant between the two units to transfer heat for cooling or heating.

d. Thermostat: The thermostat controls the system by sensing the room's temperature and signaling the system to start or stop heating or cooling when the temperature reaches the set point.

Types of Split Systems

a. Cooling-Only Split Systems: These systems are designed solely for air conditioning. They cool the air inside a space by removing heat and expelling it outside. The outdoor unit contains the compressor and condenser, while the indoor unit contains the evaporator coil and blower fan.

b. Heat Pump Split Systems: A heat pump split system can both heat and cool the air. In the summer, it works like a regular air conditioner, cooling the indoor space by removing heat. In winter, it reverses the process and extracts heat from the outdoor air (even in cold temperatures) to warm the indoor space.

c. Ductless Mini-Split Systems: These are a type of split system that does not use traditional ducts to distribute air. Instead, small indoor units are installed in each room or zone, and each unit has its own temperature controls. This makes ductless mini-splits ideal for homes without ductwork or for room-by-room temperature control.

Advantages of Split Systems

a. Energy Efficiency: Split systems are more energy-efficient compared to older HVAC systems because they don't have the energy losses that occur in ductwork. Without ducts, there is less chance for air leaks or energy loss, making the system more efficient.

b. Flexibility in Installation: The indoor and outdoor units can be installed in various configurations. The indoor unit can be mounted on walls, ceilings, or even placed on the floor, while the outdoor unit can be placed outside, making it flexible for different space requirements.

c. Zoning Capability: Some split systems, especially ductless mini-split systems, allow for zoning. This means you can control the temperature in individual rooms or areas, which is great for personal comfort and energy savings. For example, you can keep the bedroom cooler at night while leaving the living room warmer during the day.

d. Quiet Operation: Split systems are generally quieter than traditional HVAC systems because the noisy components, like the compressor and condenser, are located outside the home. Inside, the fan and air handling components are usually much quieter.

e. Easy Installation: Since there is no need for ductwork, the installation process is often quicker and less invasive compared to other HVAC systems. This can reduce both installation time and costs.

Disadvantages of Split Systems

a. Initial Cost: While split systems can be more affordable than central HVAC systems, they can still have a relatively high upfront cost, especially if you're installing multiple indoor units in different rooms.

b. Limited Heating Capacity in Extreme Cold: Heat pump split systems can struggle to extract enough heat from the outdoor air in very cold climates. While they work well in mild winter conditions, additional heating sources might be needed in regions with severe winters.

c. Aesthetic Impact: The indoor unit, which is typically wall-mounted, might not blend seamlessly with the room's decor. However, there are various models that are designed to be more aesthetically pleasing.

Maintaining a Split System

To ensure that a split system runs efficiently, regular maintenance is required:

i. Clean or replace air filters: Dirty filters reduce airflow and efficiency. Regularly cleaning or replacing the filters helps maintain air quality and system performance.

ii. Check refrigerant levels: Low refrigerant can reduce the system's cooling or heating capacity. A technician can check and refill the refrigerant as needed.

iii. Clean the indoor and outdoor units: Dust and debris can accumulate in the evaporator and condenser coils, reducing efficiency. Cleaning the coils helps maintain good airflow.

iv. Inspect and clean the condensate drain: Over time, the drain can get clogged with dirt or algae, so it should be cleared to prevent water damage.

Split systems are an efficient and flexible solution for heating and cooling a home or building. Whether you choose a traditional cooling-only split system, a heat pump version for year-round comfort, or a ductless mini-split system for zoning, these systems offer reliable performance and energy savings. Regular maintenance and proper installation ensure that your split system operates at its best, providing consistent comfort in your home.

3.3 Packaged Systems in HVAC

A packaged HVAC system is another type of heating, ventilation, and air conditioning system commonly used in both residential and commercial buildings. Unlike split systems, where the indoor and outdoor units are separate, a packaged system combines all the components into one single unit. This unit is typically placed outside or on the roof of a building, making it a great option when indoor space is limited or when you want a compact system.

What Is a Packaged System

In a packaged HVAC system, all the components needed to heat, cool, and circulate air are contained within one unit. These systems include the furnace, air conditioner, and sometimes a heat pump, all in one convenient package. The system works by using a single outdoor unit to perform all functions of heating and cooling, which makes installation and maintenance easier.

How Does a Packaged System Work?

A packaged system works by taking in outdoor air, conditioning it, and then circulating it throughout the building. Here's a step-by-step breakdown of how it works:

a. Cooling Mode: The air is drawn into the packaged unit, where the air conditioning components cool it by removing heat using a refrigerant. The cooled air is then sent through ducts into the building.

b. Heating Mode: If the system includes a furnace or heat pump, it can also provide heating. The furnace heats the air inside the unit, or the heat pump extracts heat from the outside air and transfers it indoors. The heated air is then distributed throughout the building through ducts.

c. Ventilation: The packaged system also helps circulate the air inside the building. This process ensures that fresh air is brought in and stale air is removed, maintaining proper airflow and air quality.

Key Components of a Packaged HVAC System

i. Compressor: The compressor is a key part of the air conditioning function. It compresses the refrigerant and circulates it through the system to remove heat from the air.

ii. Evaporator Coil: The evaporator coil absorbs heat from the air and works with the refrigerant to cool the air. It is typically located inside the packaged unit.

iii. Condenser Coil: The condenser coil releases the absorbed heat outside, usually in the outdoor unit of the packaged system.

iv. Blower Fan: The blower fan circulates the air through the system, ensuring that conditioned air is pushed through the ducts and into the rooms.

v. Thermostat: A thermostat is used to control the temperature by signaling the packaged system to turn on or off when the desired temperature is reached.

Types of Packaged HVAC Systems

i. Packaged Air Conditioners: These systems only provide cooling. The packaged unit houses both the evaporator coil and the condenser coil, cooling the air and then sending it into the building through ducts.

ii. Packaged Heat Pump Systems: These systems provide both heating and cooling. The heat pump in the packaged unit can either heat or cool the air depending on the season, making it a year-round solution for temperature control.

iii. Packaged Gas and Electric Systems: In these systems, the packaged unit contains both a gas furnace for heating and an electric air conditioner for cooling. The furnace heats the air in the winter, while the air conditioner cools it in the summer.

iv. Packaged Dual-Fuel Systems: These systems combine a gas furnace for heating with an electric heat pump for cooling. They switch between the two heating sources depending on which are more efficient for the current temperature.

Advantages of Packaged Systems

i. Space-Saving: Since all the components are combined into one unit, packaged systems take up less space indoors. This is ideal for buildings where space is limited or where you don't want bulky equipment taking up valuable space inside.

ii. Easy Installation: Packaged systems are easier to install compared to split systems because everything is contained in a single unit. There's no need for separate indoor and outdoor units or complex ductwork, which makes installation quicker and less expensive.

iii. Reduced Indoor Noise: With the unit placed outside or on the roof, packaged systems reduce the noise inside the building. The noisy components, such as the compressor and condenser, are located outdoors, so the indoor space remains quiet.

iv. Convenient Maintenance: Maintenance and repairs are simpler because everything is in one place. The technician only needs to service one unit, which can be accessed from the outside. This reduces the time and cost of maintenance.

v. Energy Efficiency: Packaged systems are often energy-efficient because the components are housed together in one unit, making the system easier to maintain and operate efficiently. Many newer models are designed to reduce energy consumption while maintaining comfort.

Disadvantages of Packaged Systems

a. Limited Capacity: Packaged systems are typically designed for smaller to medium-sized buildings. For larger spaces or multi-story buildings, they may not be as effective as central HVAC systems, which can handle more extensive heating and cooling needs.

b. Outdoor Placement: Since the system is usually installed outside or on the roof, it's exposed to weather conditions. Extreme temperatures, storms, or other environmental factors can sometimes affect the performance of the system.

c. Initial Cost: Although the installation is simpler, packaged systems can have a higher initial cost compared to split systems, especially for systems that include both heating and cooling.

d. Maintenance Access: While maintenance is generally easier, accessing the system for repairs may be more challenging if it is installed on the roof or in a hard-to-reach location. Special equipment may be required for servicing the system.

Maintaining a Packaged HVAC System

To ensure that a packaged HVAC system runs efficiently, regular maintenance is required. Here are some important tasks to keep in mind:

a. Change or clean filters: Dirty filters can reduce airflow and make the system work harder. Regularly clean or replace the filters to maintain good air quality and system performance.

b. Inspect the refrigerant levels: Low refrigerant levels can affect the cooling or heating capacity. A technician can check and refill refrigerant if needed.

c. Clean the coils and components: Dust and debris can accumulate on the evaporator and condenser coils, reducing efficiency. Cleaning the coils regularly can improve performance.

d. Check the blower fan: Ensure that the blower fan is working properly to circulate air throughout the system.

e. Annual inspections: It is important to have the system checked annually by a professional to ensure that it is working properly and to catch any potential problems early.

A packaged HVAC system is a convenient and space-saving solution for heating and cooling a building. It combines all the necessary components into a single unit, making it easier to install and maintain. While it may have some limitations in terms of capacity and exposure to outdoor elements, packaged systems are a great choice for homes and buildings that need efficient temperature control without taking up indoor space. Regular maintenance ensures the system performs efficiently and continues to provide comfort throughout the year.

3.4 Hybrid HVAC Systems

A Hybrid HVAC System is a type of heating, ventilation, and air conditioning system that combines two different technologies to provide both heating and cooling. It typically uses a heat pump for cooling and mild heating, and a furnace (usually gas-powered) for additional heating when the temperature drops significantly. This combination allows the system to switch between the two sources of heating and cooling depending on the weather, ensuring the home stays comfortable and energy-efficient throughout the year.

How Does a Hybrid HVAC System Work

Hybrid systems work by using both a heat pump and a furnace to manage indoor temperatures. Here is a breakdown of how it functions:

a. Cooling Mode: During the summer, the system works like a typical air conditioner. The heat pump removes heat from the inside of the home and expels it outside, cooling the air indoors.

b. Heating Mode: In mild winter weather, the heat pump can still be used to heat the home. It works by extracting heat from the outdoor air (even in cold temperatures) and bringing it indoors. When the temperature drops too low for the heat pump to be effective (usually below freezing), the system automatically switches to the furnace to provide the necessary warmth. The furnace uses gas, oil, or electricity to generate heat and distribute it throughout the home.

c. Automatic Switching: One of the main benefits of a hybrid system is that it can automatically switch between the heat pump and the furnace based on the temperature outside. The system chooses the most energy-efficient option to maintain a comfortable indoor temperature.

Key Components of a Hybrid HVAC System

a. Heat Pump: The heat pump is the heart of the hybrid system for heating and cooling. It extracts heat from the outdoor air and transfers it indoors in the winter, and it removes heat from indoor air to cool the space during the summer.

b. Furnace: The furnace is used for heating when the heat pump cannot efficiently do so, typically in extremely cold temperatures. Furnaces usually run on natural gas, electricity, or oil.

c. Thermostat: The thermostat controls the system, maintaining the desired indoor temperature. In a hybrid system, the thermostat also helps determine when to switch between the heat pump and the furnace based on outdoor conditions.

d. Ductwork: Hybrid systems use a network of ducts to distribute heated or cooled air throughout the building. The ducts carry the conditioned air from the heat pump or furnace into each room.

Advantages of Hybrid HVAC Systems

a. Energy Efficiency: Hybrid systems are highly energy-efficient because they use the most appropriate and cost-effective heating or cooling method based on the weather. The heat pump is much more energy-efficient than a furnace, especially when the temperature is moderate. The furnace is only used when absolutely necessary.

b. Cost Savings: By automatically switching between the heat pump and the furnace, hybrid systems can lower energy costs over time. Heat pumps consume less electricity compared to furnaces, which can lead to reduced heating bills, especially in regions with mild winters.

c. Year-Round Comfort: Hybrid systems provide both heating and cooling, making them an all-in-one solution for year-round comfort. The heat pump can cool the house in the summer and heat it in the winter (in mild temperatures), while the furnace provides additional heat when it gets really cold.

d. Environmental Benefits: Since hybrid systems use electricity (for the heat pump) and natural gas or renewable energy (for the furnace), they can have a smaller carbon footprint compared to traditional heating systems that rely solely on fossil fuels. The heat pump is especially environmentally friendly because it doesn't burn fuel to generate heat.

e. Improved Indoor Air Quality: Hybrid systems, like other HVAC systems, help circulate air throughout the home, which can improve indoor air quality by filtering out dust, allergens, and pollutants. Some models also come with additional filtration options to further improve air quality.

Disadvantages of Hybrid HVAC Systems

i. Higher Initial Cost: He upfront cost of installing a hybrid HVAC system is generally higher than that of a standard heat pump or furnace alone, because it requires both a heat pump and a furnace. This initial investment can be a barrier for some homeowners.

ii. Complex Installation: Installing a hybrid system can be more complex and require additional space for both the heat pump and furnace. It may also require specialized installation, which could lead to higher labor costs.

iii. Maintenance: Like any HVAC system, hybrid systems need regular maintenance. Both the heat pump and the furnace should be checked periodically to ensure that they are running efficiently. If either component fails, it could disrupt the balance of the system and lead to higher repair costs.

iv. Not Ideal for Extremely Cold Climates: While the furnace provides supplemental heat in colder weather, hybrid systems might not be as effective in extremely cold climates where the furnace is needed more often. In such areas, a furnace-only system or a more powerful heating solution might be more suitable.

Maintaining a Hybrid HVAC System

To ensure that a hybrid HVAC system works efficiently, regular maintenance is important. Here are some tips:

a. Change air filters: Regularly change or clean the filters to maintain good air quality and system efficiency.

b. Inspect and clean the heat pump and furnace: Regularly has a technician inspect both the heat pump and furnace to ensure that they are working properly.

c. Check refrigerant levels: If the refrigerant level in the heat pump is low, it can affect the system's ability to cool or heat efficiently.

d. Clean the coils: Dirt and debris can build up on the evaporator and condenser coils in the heat pump, reducing its efficiency. Regular cleaning helps keep it running smoothly.

e. Annual inspections: Schedule professional annual maintenance to ensure both the heat pump and furnace are in good working condition.

A Hybrid HVAC System is an energy-efficient and cost-effective solution for heating and cooling a home. By combining a heat pump and a furnace, hybrid systems can provide year-round comfort while using the most efficient method for the current weather. Although they may have a higher initial cost, they can lead to long-term savings by reducing energy consumption. Proper maintenance is key to keeping the system running efficiently, ensuring both heating and cooling needs are met throughout the year.

Part 2: Heating Systems

Chapter Four: Overview of Heating in HVAC

Heating is one of the most important functions of an HVAC (Heating, Ventilation, and Air Conditioning) system. It helps maintain a comfortable indoor temperature during cold weather and ensures that homes and buildings stay warm and cozy. In HVAC systems, heating is typically achieved through different types of equipment that work together to warm up the air or space. These systems are designed to generate heat and distribute it evenly throughout the space to ensure a consistent and comfortable environment.

How Does Heating Work in HVAC

Heating in an HVAC system generally works by generating heat and then distributing it through the building via air or water. The key steps involved in heating are:

a. Heat Generation: The heating system starts by generating heat. This is done through various equipment, such as furnaces, boilers, or heat pumps. The heat is produced using different energy sources like electricity, natural gas, or oil.

b. Heat Distribution: Once the heat is generated, it needs to be distributed throughout the building. The distribution can be done using air (in systems like forced air systems) or water (in systems like radiant heating). The warm air or water is sent into rooms through ducts, pipes, or radiators, maintaining a comfortable indoor temperature.

c. Temperature Regulation: The thermostat controls the temperature by sensing the indoor air temperature and regulating the heating system. It turns the system on or off to maintain the set temperature, ensuring the space is not too hot or too cold.

Benefits of Heating in HVAC Systems

a. Comfort: Heating systems provide comfort by maintaining a warm and consistent indoor temperature, making homes and buildings comfortable to live and work in, even during the coldest months.

b. Energy Efficiency: Many modern HVAC heating systems are designed to be energy-efficient, which helps reduce energy consumption and lower heating bills. Systems like heat pumps and high-efficiency furnaces can provide warmth while using less energy.

c. Health: Heating helps maintain a healthy indoor environment by preventing pipes from freezing, reducing humidity levels, and keeping mold or mildew growth in check. Some systems also include air filtration to improve indoor air quality.

d. Cost Savings: By using an efficient heating system, homeowners can save money on their energy bills. Investing in a high-efficiency system or upgrading an old system can result in significant savings over time

e. Heating is a critical component of any HVAC system, providing warmth and comfort during colder months. There are various types of heating systems, including furnaces, boilers, heat pumps, radiant heating, and space heaters, each with its own benefits and limitations. By selecting the right heating system for your home or building, you can enjoy a warm and comfortable environment while also saving on energy costs. Regular maintenance is also key to keeping your heating system running efficiently and effectively.

4.1 : Types of Heating Systems

A. Forced Air Heating: A Common Type of Heating System

Forced Air Heating is one of the most widely used heating systems in HVAC. It works by heating air and distributing it throughout a building using ducts and vents. This type of system is known for its efficiency, reliability, and ability to quickly heat a space. It is commonly found in homes, offices, and other buildings.

How Does Forced Air Heating Work

The forced air heating system follows a simple process to warm your space. Here is how it works:

a. Heat Generation: The system begins by generating heat. This is typically done using a furnace, which burns natural gas, propane, oil, or uses electricity to create heat. In some systems, a heat pump may also be used as the heat source.

b. Air Heating: Once the heat is generated, the furnace heats the air. This is done as the air passes over a heat exchanger, a component that transfers the generated heat to the air without mixing with combustion gases.

c. Air Distribution: After the air is heated, a blower fan pushes the warm air into the ductwork system. The ducts carry the warm air to different rooms or zones in the building. The air is released into the rooms through vents or registers.

d. Temperature Control: The system is controlled by a thermostat, which monitors the indoor temperature. When the room temperature drops below the thermostat's setting, the system turns on to heat the air and distributes it. Once the desired temperature is reached, the thermostat signals the system to stop heating.

e. Air Recirculation: Cool air from the rooms is pulled back into the system through return air ducts, where it is reheated and recalculated. This continuous process ensures that the indoor space remains warm and comfortable.

Key Components of a Forced Air Heating System

a. Furnace: The furnace is the core of the system. It generates heat using gas, electricity, or oil and transfers that heat to the air.

b. Heat Exchanger: The heat exchanger is where the air is warmed. It absorbs the heat from the furnace and transfers it to the air without mixing combustion gases with the airflow.

c. Blower Fan: The blower fan pushes the heated air into the ductwork system, ensuring it reaches all areas of the building.

d. Ductwork: The ductwork is a network of insulated pipes that carry warm air from the furnace to the rooms and return cool air back to the furnace for reheating.

e. Thermostat: The thermostat is the control center of the system. It allows users to set the desired temperature and automatically turns the system on or off to maintain that temperature.

f. Vents and Registers: These are the openings in the walls, floors, or ceilings through which the warm air enters the rooms. Return air vents allow cool air to be pulled back into the system.

Advantages of Forced Air Heating

a. Quick Heating: Forced air systems heat up quickly, making them an efficient option for rapidly warming up a space.

b. Even Heat Distribution: With a well-designed ductwork system, the heat is evenly distributed throughout the entire building.

c. Energy Efficiency: Modern forced air systems are highly energy-efficient, especially those with high-efficiency furnaces or heat pumps.

d. Compatibility with Air Conditioning: Forced air systems can be combined with central air conditioning, allowing a single ductwork system to be used for both heating and cooling.

e. Air Filtration: These systems can include air filters or air purifiers, which help remove dust, allergens, and pollutants from the air, improving indoor air quality.

f. Customizable Temperature Control: With zoned heating options, different areas of the home or building can be set to different temperatures, increasing comfort and energy savings.

Disadvantages of Forced Air Heating

a. Ductwork Maintenance: The ducts need to be cleaned regularly to prevent dust buildup and ensure good air quality. Leaks in ducts can also lead to heat loss, reducing efficiency.

b. Noise: The blower fan and airflow through the ducts can produce noise, which may be noticeable in some homes or buildings.

c. Uneven Heating in Poorly Designed Systems: If the ductwork is not properly designed or insulated, some rooms may become too hot while others remain cold.

d. Air Movement Can Spread Allergens: While filters can improve air quality, the movement of air can still stir up dust or allergens, which may be problematic for sensitive individuals.

e. Higher Initial Cost: Installing a forced air system with ductwork can be more expensive upfront compared to simpler heating solutions like space heaters.

Is Forced Air Heating Right for You

Forced air heating is an excellent option for homes and buildings that need efficient, fast, and reliable heating. It is especially ideal if you already have ductwork in place for central air conditioning or if you're building a new home. However, if you're concerned about noise or air circulation issues, you might need to consider proper system design and maintenance.

Tips for Maintaining a Forced Air Heating System

a. Change Air Filters Regularly: Dirty air filters can reduce airflow and make the system work harder, lowering efficiency. Replace filters every 1–3 months.

b. Inspect Ductwork: Have a professional inspect the ducts for leaks or blockages and clean them regularly to maintain efficiency.

c. Schedule Annual Maintenance: A professional HVAC technician should check the system annually to ensure all components are functioning correctly and efficiently.

d. Seal and Insulate Ducts: Properly sealed and insulated ducts prevent heat loss and improve energy efficiency.

e. Upgrade to a Programmable Thermostat: A programmable thermostat can help optimize heating schedules, reducing energy consumption and costs

Forced air heating is a popular and effective way to heat homes and buildings. It provides fast, even heating and can be combined with air conditioning for year-round comfort. While it requires proper maintenance and ductwork care, its advantages, including energy efficiency and air filtration, make it a great choice for many homeowners. By keeping the system well-maintained, you can ensure it operates efficiently and keeps your indoor space warm and cozy during the cold months.

B. Radiant Heating: A Unique Type of Heating System in HVAC

Radiant heating is a type of heating system that warms a space by directly heating surfaces, such as floors, walls, or ceilings, rather than heating the air. This method relies on the natural process of radiation, where heat is transferred from warm surfaces to people and objects in the room. Radiant heating creates a comfortable, even warmth that feels natural, similar to the way the sun warms the ground.

How Does Radiant Heating Work

Radiant heating systems work by using either water or electricity to generate heat. The heat is then transferred through surfaces to provide warmth. Here is how the process works:

a. Heat Generation: In hydronic systems (water-based), a boiler heats water and circulates it through pipes installed beneath floors, inside walls, or ceilings. In electric systems, electrical wires or mats embedded in floors, walls, or ceilings generate heat.

b. Heat Transfer: The heated surfaces, like floors or walls, radiate warmth directly to people and objects in the room. This eliminates the need for fans or blowers, resulting in quiet and even heating.

c. Temperature Regulation: Radiant heating systems are controlled by a thermostat that allows you to adjust the temperature to your preference. Some systems also allow for zoning, meaning different areas of the home can be set to different temperatures.

Types of Radiant Heating Systems

a. Hydronic Radiant Heating: This is the most common and energy-efficient type of radiant heating. It uses a boiler to heat water, which is then circulated through a network of tubes or pipes installed beneath the floor. Ideal For: Larger homes or buildings, as it are cost-effective for heating large spaces. Energy Source: Can use natural gas, oil, or electricity to heat the water.

b. Electric Radiant Heating: This system uses electrical heating elements, such as wires or mats, installed beneath the surface to generate heat. Ideal For: Smaller spaces, individual rooms (like bathrooms), or areas where hydronic systems are not practical. Energy Source: Electricity.

c. Radiant Panels: These systems use panels mounted on walls or ceilings to radiate heat. Radiant panels are usually electric and provide quick heating for specific areas. Ideal For: Supplemental heating in rooms where extra warmth is needed.

Advantages of Radiant Heating

a. Comfortable and Even Heat: Radiant heating provides consistent warmth without hot or cold spots. Since it heats surfaces rather than air, the warmth feels natural and soothing.

b. Energy Efficiency: Radiant heating is energy-efficient because it eliminates heat loss caused by air circulation (common in forced air systems). Hydroid systems, in particular, can be very cost-effective for larger spaces.

c. Quiet Operation: Unlike forced air systems, radiant heating operates silently since there are no fans or blowers involved.

d. Improved Indoor Air Quality: Radiant systems don't rely on blowing air, which means they don't stir up dust, allergens, or pollutants. This makes them a great choice for people with allergies or respiratory issues.

e. Invisible System: Radiant heating systems are installed under floors, inside walls, or ceilings, so they do not take up space or interfere with the design of a room.

f. Customizable Zones: Many radiant systems allow for zoning, meaning you can heat specific areas or rooms independently, reducing energy usage and costs.

Disadvantages of Radiant Heating

a. Higher Installation Costs: Radiant heating systems, especially hydronic ones, can be expensive to install, as they require significant labor and materials.

b. Slow Heating: Radiant systems take longer to heat a space compared to forced air systems because they rely on heating surfaces gradually.

c. Limited Cooling Capability: Radiant heating systems only provide heating. If cooling is also needed, a separate air conditioning system must be installed.

d. Repairs Can Be Difficult: Since the system is embedded beneath floors or inside walls, accessing and repairing components can be challenging and costly.

e. Energy Source Dependence: Electric radiant systems can be expensive to operate in areas where electricity costs are high.

Where Is Radiant Heating Used

Radiant heating is versatile and can be used in various settings. Here are some examples:

a. Residential Homes: Radiant heating is popular in homes, especially in rooms like bathrooms and kitchens where warm floors are particularly desirable.

b. Commercial Buildings: It is often used in offices, warehouses, or workshops where consistent heating is needed without blowing air.

c. Outdoor Spaces: Radiant heating can also be installed outdoors, such as in driveways or patios, to melt snow or provide warmth in colder climates.

Installation Considerations

a. Flooring Material: Radiant heating works best with flooring materials that conduct heat well, such as tile, concrete, or stone. While it can be used with wood or carpet, these materials may reduce efficiency.

b. Retrofitting vs. New Construction: Radiant heating is easier to install in new construction projects. Retrofitting an existing home can be more complicated and expensive.

c. Insulation: Proper insulation is essential to maximize the efficiency of radiant heating. Insulation beneath the heating system ensures that heat rises into the room rather than being lost below.

Advantages of Radiant Heating in Bathrooms and Kitchens

Radiant heating is particularly popular in bathrooms and kitchens for these reasons:

i. Warm Floors: Walking barefoot on a warm floor in cold weather is a luxurious comfort, especially in tiled areas like bathrooms.

ii. Humidity Control: Radiant systems help keep these spaces warm and dry, reducing the risk of mold and mildew.

Is Radiant Heating Right for You

Radiant heating is an excellent choice if you value quiet, energy-efficient, and even heat. It is particularly ideal for those with allergies or respiratory issues, as it doesn't circulate air. While the upfront cost may be higher, the long-term benefits, including comfort and energy savings, often outweigh the initial investment. It is especially well-suited for new construction projects or major renovations.

Radiant heating is a modern and efficient way to heat a home or building. By warming surfaces instead of the air, it provides consistent, comfortable warmth without the noise or air movement associated with other heating systems. Although it may involve higher installation costs, its energy efficiency, health benefits, and comfort make it a worthwhile investment for many homeowners.

C. Heat pumps

Heat pumps are a type of heating system in HVAC that works by transferring heat from one place to another. Unlike traditional heating systems like furnaces or boilers that generate heat by burning fuel, heat pumps move existing heat from the outside environment into your home to warm it up. They are versatile because they can also work in reverse to cool your home during summer, making them both a heating and cooling system.

How Heat Pumps Work

Heat pumps use a process that relies on a refrigerant, coils, and a compressor to transfer heat. Here is how they work in heating mode:

a. Heat Absorption: Even in cold weather, there is some heat present in the air, ground, or water outside. The heat pump extracts this heat using an outdoor coil.

b. Compression: The refrigerant, a special fluid inside the heat pump, absorbs the outdoor heat. The heat pump's compressor then compresses the refrigerant, which increases its temperature significantly.

c. Heat Release: The heated refrigerant is sent to the indoor coil, where it releases its heat into the home through a blower or radiant heating system.

d. Cycle Repeats: Once the heat is released, the refrigerant cools down and is sent back outdoors to absorb more heat, repeating the cycle.

This efficient process of transferring heat rather than generating it makes heat pumps highly energy-efficient.

Types of Heat Pumps

There are three main types of heat pumps, each using a different heat source:

a. Air-Source Heat Pumps: These are the most common type of heat pumps. They draw heat from the outdoor air and transfer it into your home. They work well in moderate climates, but newer models are designed to operate efficiently even in colder temperatures. Air-source heat pumps are easier and less expensive to install compared to other types.

b. Ground-Source (Geothermal) Heat Pumps: These pumps extract heat from the ground, where the temperature is more stable than the air. Pipes are buried underground, and the heat pump transfers heat from the ground to your home. Ground-source systems are more efficient than air-source systems and work well in colder climates. However, they are expensive to install because they require digging or drilling into the ground.

c. Water-Source Heat Pumps: These heat pumps use a nearby water source, like a lake, pond, or well, to extract heat. They are highly efficient but are limited to properties that have access to a suitable water source.

Advantages of Heat Pumps

i. Energy Efficiency: Heat pumps use electricity to move heat rather than generate it, making them much more energy-efficient than traditional heating systems. They can provide up to three times more heat than the energy they consume.

ii. Year-Round Comfort: Heat pumps work as both heating and cooling systems, eliminating the need for separate air conditioners or heaters.

iii. Lower Carbon Footprint: Since they don't rely on burning fossil fuels, heat pumps are an environmentally friendly option.

iv. Even Heating: They provide consistent and even heating throughout your home without creating hot or cold spots.

v. Quiet Operation: Modern heat pumps are designed to operate quietly, making them ideal for homes.

Disadvantages of Heat Pumps

i. Higher Initial Cost: Installing a heat pump can be more expensive upfront compared to traditional heating systems.

ii. Efficiency in Cold Climates: Air-source heat pumps may struggle in extremely cold temperatures, though newer models with advanced technology are addressing this issue.

iii. Electricity Dependence: Heat pumps rely entirely on electricity, which can make them costly to operate in areas where electricity prices are high.

iv. Complex Installation: Ground-source and water-source heat pumps require specialized installation, which can be time-consuming and expensive.

Where Heat Pumps Are Best Suited

Heat pumps are ideal for areas with moderate climates where extreme cold is not common. However, modern heat pumps, especially geothermal ones, can work well even in colder regions when paired with supplemental heating systems. They are also great for energy-conscious homeowners who want a single system for heating and cooling.

Maintenance and Care

To keep a heat pump running efficiently, regular maintenance is necessary:

i. Clean or replace air filters every 1–3 months.

ii. Schedule annual professional maintenance to inspect the refrigerant levels, clean coils, and check for any issues.

iii. Ensure outdoor units are free of debris like leaves or snow.

Heat pumps are an excellent HVAC solution for efficient heating and cooling. By transferring heat rather than generating it, they offer a cost-effective and environmentally friendly option for year-round comfort. Whether you choose an air-source, ground-source, or water-source heat pump, they are a reliable choice for homes and businesses looking to reduce energy consumption and lower their environmental impact.

D. Geothermal Heating Systems: A Type of Heating System in HVAC

Geothermal heating systems, also known as ground-source heating systems, are a highly energy-efficient and eco-friendly way to heat homes and buildings. These systems work by tapping into the stable temperature of the earth beneath the surface to provide heating. Unlike traditional heating systems that rely on burning fuel or generating heat directly, geothermal systems use the earth's natural heat, which is a renewable and sustainable energy source.

How Geothermal Heating Systems Work

Geothermal heating systems utilize the fact that the temperature underground remains relatively constant throughout the year, regardless of the weather above. This stable ground temperature, typically between 45°F and 75°F (7°C to 24°C), provides an efficient source of heat. Here's how the system works:

a. Heat Collection: A series of pipes, called a ground loop, is buried underground. These pipes are filled with a fluid (usually water or a water-antifreeze mixture) that circulates through the system. The fluid absorbs heat from the ground.

b. Heat Transfer: The heated fluid is pumped into a heat pump located inside the building. The heat pump extracts the heat from the fluid and compresses it, raising its temperature even further.

c. Heat Distribution: The high-temperature heat is then distributed throughout the building using a forced-air system (ducts and vents) or a radiant heating system (pipes under the floors).

d. Cycle Repeats: Once the heat is extracted, the cooled fluid is sent back into the ground loop to absorb more heat, and the cycle continues.

In the summer, the process can be reversed, allowing the system to cool the building by transferring heat from inside the home back into the ground. This makes geothermal systems a year-round solution for both heating and cooling.

Types of Geothermal Heating Systems

There are several types of geothermal systems, depending on how the ground loop is installed:

a. Closed-Loop Systems: In these systems, the same fluid circulates through a continuous loop of pipes buried in the ground. There are two common configurations:

i. Horizontal Loops: Pipes are laid out in shallow trenches. This is a cost-effective option if there is enough land available.

ii. Vertical Loops: Pipes are drilled deep into the ground. This is ideal for properties with limited space but involves higher installation costs.

b. Open-Loop Systems: These systems use a natural water source, like a well or pond, to circulate water through the system. After the heat is extracted, the water is returned to the source. Open-loop systems are efficient but require access to a sufficient water supply.

c. Pond/Lake Systems: If a large body of water is available nearby, pipes can be submerged in the water to absorb heat. This type is usually less expensive to install compared to other closed-loop systems.

Advantages of Geothermal Heating Systems

a. Energy Efficiency: Geothermal systems are one of the most energy-efficient heating systems available. They can deliver up to 4-5 units of heat for every unit of electricity they use, making them much more efficient than traditional systems.

b. Environmentally Friendly: Since they use the earth's natural heat, geothermal systems reduce the need for fossil fuels and lower greenhouse gas emissions. This makes them an excellent choice for environmentally conscious homeowners.

c. Lower Operating Costs: While the upfront installation cost can be high, geothermal systems have low operating costs. They can significantly reduce heating and cooling bills over time.

d. Longevity: The underground components, such as the ground loop, can last 50 years or more, while the indoor heat pump typically lasts 20-25 years with proper maintenance.

e. Quiet Operation: Geothermal systems operate quietly since there are no loud fans or outdoor units like in traditional HVAC systems.

f. Consistent Comfort: These systems provide even, consistent heating throughout the home, without temperature fluctuations or cold spots.

g. Dual Functionality: Geothermal systems can provide both heating and cooling, eliminating the need for separate systems.

Disadvantages of Geothermal Heating Systems

a. High Installation Cost: The upfront cost for geothermal systems is higher than most other heating systems, primarily due to the cost of drilling or trenching for the ground loop.

b. Land and Space Requirements: Horizontal loop systems require significant land area, which might not be feasible for smaller properties.

c. Complex Installation: Installing a geothermal system requires specialized knowledge and equipment, which can make the process more complex and time-consuming.

d. Water Source Dependence: Open-loop systems depend on a consistent and clean water source, which may not be available in all locations.

e. Potential Ground Disruption: Installing the ground loop involves digging or drilling, which can disrupt the landscape and require restoration work.

Where Geothermal Heating Systems Are Used

Geothermal systems are an excellent option for homes and buildings in a wide range of climates. They are especially beneficial in areas with stable ground temperatures and sufficient land for installation. They are commonly used in residential homes, commercial buildings, and even in schools and hospitals.

Maintenance Requirements

Geothermal systems require minimal maintenance compared to traditional systems:
i. Ground Loop: The underground pipes are highly durable and usually maintenance-free.
ii. Heat Pump: Regular maintenance, such as cleaning filters and checking refrigerant levels, ensures efficient operation.
iii. Inspections: Annual professional inspections can help identify and fix any potential issues early.
Geothermal heating systems are a smart and sustainable choice for heating and cooling homes or buildings. By harnessing the earth's stable temperatures, they offer unmatched energy efficiency, lower operating costs, and environmental benefits. While the initial installation cost may be higher, the long-term savings and reliability make geothermal systems a worthwhile investment. They are ideal for homeowners looking for a quiet, consistent, and eco-friendly HVAC solution.

4.2 Energy Sources for Heating

In HVAC systems, heating relies on different energy sources to generate warmth for homes and buildings. Heating systems in HVAC rely on different energy sources to generate warmth. Three of the most common energy sources are **natural gas**, **electricity**, and **oil**. Each type of energy source has unique features, advantages, and drawbacks. Let us take a closer look at how these sources are used in HVAC heating systems.

1. Gas Heating: Gas heating systems use natural gas or propane as a fuel source. This is one of the most common and cost-effective ways to heat homes and buildings.

How It Works:

a. Natural gas or propane is burned in a furnace or boiler.

b. The heat generated warms air (in a furnace) or water (in a boiler).

c. In a furnace, the warm air is circulated through ducts to heat the home.

d. In a boiler, hot water or steam is distributed through radiators or pipes for radiant heating.

Advantages

a. Cost-Effective: Natural gas is usually cheaper than electricity or oil in areas where it is available.

b. High Efficiency: Modern gas heating systems, like high-efficiency condensing furnaces, can convert up to 98% of the fuel into usable heat.

c. Quick Heating: Gas systems can quickly heat a home, making them suitable for colder climates. Widely Available:

d. Natural gas is readily available in most urban and suburban areas.

Disadvantages:

a. Requires a Gas Line: Homes without access to natural gas need to rely on propane, which requires a storage tank.

b. Safety Concerns: Leaks in gas lines can be dangerous, so regular maintenance and inspections are necessary.

c. Environmental Impact: Burning natural gas releases carbon dioxide, contributing to greenhouse gas emissions.

2. Electric Heating

Electric heating systems use electricity to generate heat. These systems are versatile and include electric furnaces, baseboard heaters, and heat pumps.

How It Works:

a. In electric furnaces, heating elements (coils) convert electricity into heat.

b. The heat is then distributed through ducts and vents, similar to gas furnaces.

c. Heat pumps work by transferring heat from outside air or the ground into the home using electricity.

Advantages:

a. Clean at Point of Use: Electric heating systems don't produce emissions in the home, making them environmentally friendly at the source.

b. Widely Available: Electricity is available in virtually all locations, even in remote areas where gas or oil might not be accessible.

c. Low Initial Cost: Electric heating systems are often cheaper to install than gas or oil systems.

d. Safe: There's no risk of gas leaks or carbon monoxide poisoning.

Disadvantages:

a. Higher Operating Costs: Electricity is often more expensive than natural gas, especially in colder regions where heating is used extensively.

b. Slower Heating: Electric systems may take longer to warm up a home compared to gas systems.

c. Dependence on Power Supply: Electric heating systems don't work during power outages unless there's a backup generator.

3. Oil Heating

Oil heating systems use heating oil as a fuel source. These systems are less common today but are still widely used in rural areas where natural gas is unavailable.

How It Works:

a. Heating oil is stored in a tank on the property.

b. The oil is burned in a furnace or boiler to generate heat.

c. The heat is distributed through ducts (for air heating) or pipes (for water or steam heating).

Advantages:

a. High Heat Output: Oil heating systems produce more heat per BTU (British thermal unit) than many other systems, making them effective in very cold climates.

b. Independence: Homeowners can store their own fuel, providing control over supply and delivery.

c. Reliable: Oil systems are highly durable and can last for decades with proper maintenance.

Disadvantages:

a. Higher Fuel Costs: Heating oil is typically more expensive than natural gas and can fluctuate in price.

b. Storage Tank Required: Oil heating requires a storage tank, which takes up space and needs regular inspections to prevent leaks.

c. Environmental Concerns: Burning oil produces more greenhouse gas emissions compared to gas or electricity.

d Maintenance: Oil systems require regular cleaning and maintenance to prevent soot buildup and ensure efficiency.

Key Differences Between Gas, Electric, and Oil Heating

Feature	Gas Heating	Electric Heating	Oil Heating
Fuel Source	Natural gas or propane	Electricity	Heating oil
Cost	Lower operating cost	Higher operating cost	Variable (can be high)
Efficiency	Highly efficient	Efficient but costly	Less efficient
Availability	Requires gas line	Available everywhere	Requires oil delivery
Environmental Impact	Emits CO2	Cleaner (at point of use)	Higher emissions

Which Heating System Is Best

The best heating system depends on factors like cost, fuel availability, climate, and personal preferences:

a. Gas heating is ideal for areas with access to natural gas and those looking for cost-effective, efficient heating.

b. Electric Heating works well in regions with mild winters or where electricity costs are low. It is also great for homes without access to gas or oil.

c. Oil heating is suitable for rural areas without gas lines or for homes needing high heat output in colder climates.

Gas, electric, and oil heating systems each have unique benefits and drawbacks. Gas heating is efficient and affordable but requires access to a gas line. Electric heating is clean, safe, and widely available but can be expensive to operate. Oil heating is effective in cold climates but has higher costs and environmental concerns. Choosing the right energy source depends on your location, budget, and heating needs.

4.3 Renewable Energy Sources for Heating in HVAC: Solar and Geothermal

Renewable energy sources like solar and geothermal are becoming increasingly popular for heating systems in HVAC. These energy sources are sustainable, environmentally friendly, and help reduce reliance on fossil fuels. Here is a detailed explanation of how **solar energy** and **geothermal energy** are used for heating.

1. Solar Energy for Heating

Solar energy uses the power of the sun to provide heat. It is one of the cleanest and most renewable energy sources available. In HVAC systems, solar heating typically works through solar thermal systems.

How Solar Heating Works:

a. Solar Collectors: Solar panels or collectors are installed on rooftops or open areas to capture sunlight.

b. Heat Absorption: The collectors use sunlight to heat a fluid (usually water or an antifreeze solution).

c. Heat Transfer: The heated fluid is circulated to a heat exchanger or storage tank.

d. Distribution: The heat is then distributed throughout the building using a radiant heating system (pipes under the floors or walls) or through hot water systems.

Advantages:

Eco-Friendly: Solar heating does not produce greenhouse gas emissions, making it environmentally sustainable.

a. Cost Savings: Once installed, solar energy is free to use, significantly reducing heating costs over time.

b. Renewable: The sun is an endless energy source, and solar systems work as long as sunlight is available.

c. Energy Independence: Solar heating reduces dependence on grid energy or fuel deliveries.

Disadvantages:

a. High Upfront Costs: Solar heating systems can be expensive to install.

b. Weather Dependent: Solar heating relies on sunlight, which may be limited during cloudy or winter days in some regions.

c. Space Requirements: Solar panels require enough space for installation, typically on roofs or open land.

d. Maintenance: While solar systems are low maintenance, the panels need occasional cleaning and inspection to ensure efficiency.

2. Geothermal Energy for Heating

Geothermal energy, also known as ground-source energy, uses the natural heat stored in the earth to provide heating. This energy is renewable and sustainable because the earth's temperature remains relatively constant below the surface.

How Geothermal Heating Works:

a. Ground Loop System: A system of underground pipes, called a ground loop, is installed either horizontally or vertically in the ground.

b. Heat Absorption: Fluid (usually water or a water-antifreeze mixture) circulates through the pipes and absorbs heat from the earth.

c. Heat Pump: The fluid carries the heat to a geothermal heat pump inside the building, which increases the temperature and makes it suitable for heating.

d. Heat Distribution: The heat is distributed throughout the building using ducts (for warm air) or radiant systems (for heated floors or walls).

Advantages:

a. Highly Efficient: Geothermal systems are extremely efficient, often providing 4-5 units of heat for every unit of electricity used.

b. Environmentally Friendly: Geothermal heating produces no emissions at the point of use and relies on a natural, renewable energy source.

c. Year-Round Use: Geothermal systems can provide both heating in the winter and cooling in the summer by reversing the process.

d. Low Operating Costs: Once installed, geothermal systems are inexpensive to operate compared to traditional heating systems.

e. Longevity: The underground components can last 50+ years, while the heat pump lasts about 20-25 years with proper maintenance.

Disadvantages:

a. High Installation Costs: The upfront cost of installing a geothermal system is significant, especially for the underground piping.

b. Space Requirements: Horizontal loops require a large area of land, while vertical loops involve expensive drilling.

c. Complex Installation: Geothermal systems require professional installation and specialized knowledge.

d. Initial Ground Disruption: The installation process may disrupt the landscape temporarily.

Comparison of Solar and Geothermal Heating

Feature	Solar Heating	Geothermal Heating
Energy Source	Sunlight	Earth's natural heat
Availability	Weather-dependent (requires sunlight)	Constant and reliable year-round
Efficiency	High on sunny days, less efficient on cloudy days	Highly efficient in all conditions
Installation Cost	High for solar panels and systems	High due to drilling/ground loops
Environmental Impact	Zero emissions	Zero emissions
Lifespan	20-30 years for solar panels	20-50 years, depending on components
Best For	Areas with abundant sunlight	Areas with stable ground temperatures

Why Choose Renewable Energy for Heating

Renewable energy sources like solar and geothermal are excellent options for homeowners and businesses looking to:

a. Reduce their carbon footprint.

b. Lower long-term heating costs.

c. Rely on sustainable and environmentally friendly energy sources.

d. Invest in energy systems with dual functionality.

Solar and geothermal energy are two of the most sustainable energy sources for HVAC heating systems. Solar heating uses the power of sunlight, while geothermal systems harness the earth's natural heat. Both options offer eco-friendly, efficient, and reliable solutions for heating. Although they require a higher initial investment, the long-term benefits—such as cost savings, energy independence, and environmental protection—make them an excellent choice for those looking to adopt renewable energy for their heating needs.

4.4 Choosing the Right Heating System for Your Needs

Selecting the right heating system for your home or building is an important decision. It impacts your comfort, energy efficiency, environmental footprint, and overall costs. There are several factors to consider when deciding on the best heating system for your needs. Here's a detailed guide to help you make the right choice.

Factors to Consider When Choosing a Heating System

1. Climate: The climate in your area plays a big role in determining the best heating system.

a. Cold Climates: Systems like gas furnaces, oil furnaces, and geothermal heat pumps are ideal because they provide consistent heat during freezing temperatures.

b. Mild Climates: Heat pumps and electric heating systems are more suitable because they are efficient and do not require intense heating.

c. Sunny Climates: Solar heating systems can be a great choice where sunlight is abundant.

2. Energy Source Availability: The type of fuel or energy source available in your location will narrow down your options.

a. Natural Gas: If your home has access to a natural gas line, a gas furnace or boiler may be the most cost-effective and efficient choice.

b. Electricity: For homes without gas lines, electric heating systems or heat pumps are a viable option.

c. Oil or Propane: In rural or remote areas without access to natural gas, oil or propane heating systems might be the only option.

d. Renewable Energy: Solar or geothermal systems are excellent if you want a sustainable and eco-friendly option.

3. Home Size and Layout: The size and design of your home or building affect the heating system you need.

a. Large Homes: Central heating systems like furnaces or boilers are effective for heating large spaces.

b. Small Homes or Apartments: Split systems, ductless mini-splits, or electric baseboard heaters work well for smaller areas.

c. Multi-Zone Homes: If you want to heat different areas of your home separately, ductless systems or zoned HVAC systems are good choices.

4. Energy Efficiency: Look for energy-efficient heating systems to save on utility bills and reduce environmental impact.

a. Check for AFUE (Annual Fuel Utilization Efficiency) ratings for furnaces and boilers. Higher ratings mean better efficiency.

b. For heat pumps, look at the HSPF (Heating Seasonal Performance Factor) rating.

c. Renewable energy systems like geothermal and solar heating are highly energy-efficient and sustainable.

5. Budget: Your budget will influence the type of heating system you can afford.

a. Upfront Costs: Electric heaters and gas furnaces have lower installation costs compared to geothermal and solar systems.

b. Operating Costs: Systems that use natural gas or renewable energy typically have lower running costs over time.

c. Maintenance Costs: Consider how much maintenance the system will require. For example, oil heating systems need more frequent servicing.

6. Environmental Impact: If reducing your carbon footprint is a priority, choose eco-friendly heating options.

a. Solar and geothermal systems are the most sustainable options.

b. Gas and oil systems emit greenhouse gases, but modern high-efficiency models minimize emissions.

c. Electric heating systems are clean at the point of use but depend on how electricity is generated in your area.

7. Comfort and Convenience: Consider how quickly and evenly the system can heat your space.

a. Forced air systems (like furnaces) provide quick heating and work well in cold weather.

b. Radiant heating offers consistent and even warmth but takes longer to heat up.

c. Heat pumps provide both heating and cooling, making them a versatile choice.

Types of Heating Systems and Their Suitability

i. Gas Furnaces: Best for areas with access to natural gas and cold climates. Cost-effective with quick heating.

ii. Electric Heating: Suitable for mild climates or areas without access to natural gas. Easy to install and maintain but can be costly to operate.

iii. Oil Heating: Ideal for rural areas without natural gas lines. High heat output but requires regular maintenance.

iv. Heat Pumps: Great for mild to moderate climates, offering both heating and cooling. Energy-efficient and eco-friendly.

v. Solar Heating: Perfect for sunny climates and those seeking a renewable energy option. High upfront cost but free energy from the sun.

vi. Geothermal Heating: Ideal for eco-conscious homeowners in any climate. Highly efficient with low operating costs but expensive to install.

Additional Tips for Choosing the Right Heating System

i. Consult an HVAC Professional: A licensed HVAC technician can evaluate your home's needs, recommend the best system, and ensure proper installation.

ii. Consider Long-Term Costs: Look beyond the upfront price. Factor in energy bills, maintenance, and potential repairs.

iii. Check Local Incentives: Some areas offer rebates or tax credits for energy-efficient or renewable heating systems.

iv. Size Your System Properly: An HVAC system that's too small will struggle to heat your home, while an oversized system will waste energy and money.

v. Plan for Maintenance: Regular maintenance is essential for efficiency and longevity, so choose a system that fits your lifestyle and maintenance preferences.

Choosing the right heating system depends on various factors like your climate, energy source availability, home size, and budget. Gas furnaces are great for colder regions, while heat pumps are versatile and efficient for milder climates. Solar and geothermal systems are eco-friendly but require a higher initial investment. By considering your needs, priorities, and long-term goals, you can select a heating system that keeps your home comfortable and energy-efficient for years to come.

Part 3: Ventilation Systems

Chapter Five: What is Ventilation and Why is it Important

Ventilation is the process of moving fresh air into a space and removing stale air. In an HVAC (Heating, Ventilation, and Air Conditioning) system, ventilation plays a critical role in maintaining indoor air quality, ensuring comfort, and promoting a healthy environment for occupants. It helps regulate airflow and remove contaminants, odors, moisture, and excess heat from indoor spaces.

What Does Ventilation Do

a. Brings Fresh Air In: Ventilation introduces clean, fresh air from outside into the indoor space.

b. Removes Polluted Air: It expels stale or contaminated air, which might contain dust, allergens, smoke, or harmful chemicals.

c. Controls Moisture: Proper ventilation prevents excess moisture, reducing the risk of mold and mildew.

d. Balances Temperature: It helps regulate indoor temperatures, ensuring a comfortable environment by removing excess heat or distributing conditioned air evenly.

Why is Ventilation Important in an HVAC System

a. Improves Air Quality: Ventilation reduces indoor air pollution by exchanging stale air with fresh air. This helps remove allergens, dust, and harmful gases like carbon dioxide or volatile organic compounds (VOCs).

b. Promotes Health: Poor ventilation can lead to respiratory problems, allergies, or headaches caused by pollutants or insufficient oxygen levels. Proper ventilation reduces the risk of these health issues.

c. Prevents Odors: By replacing stale air, ventilation helps eliminate unpleasant odors caused by cooking, pets, or dampness.

d. Regulates Humidity: Excess humidity can cause condensation, leading to mold and damage to walls, furniture, and electronics. Ventilation helps control moisture levels, protecting your home and belongings.

e. Enhances Comfort: A well-ventilated space feels fresher, less stuffy, and more comfortable to live or work in.

f. Supports HVAC Efficiency: Ventilation works alongside heating and cooling systems to distribute air effectively. This ensures energy-efficient operation and consistent comfort.

How Does Ventilation Work

In an HVAC system, ventilation typically works through a network of ducts, vents, and fans. Air is drawn in from the outside, filtered to remove dust and debris, and distributed throughout the building. At the same time, stale air is pushed out through exhaust vents. Advanced systems may include heat or energy recovery ventilators, which exchange heat between incoming and outgoing air to improve energy efficiency.

Ventilation is a key component of an HVAC system, ensuring that indoor air remains clean, fresh, and healthy. It removes pollutants, regulates moisture, and provides a comfortable environment. Proper ventilation is essential for maintaining good indoor air quality, promoting health, and ensuring the efficiency of your HVAC system. Whether through natural or mechanical methods, ventilation improves the overall quality of life for those inside the building.

Chapter Six: Types of Ventilation

6.1 Natural Ventilation System

Natural ventilation is a type of ventilation that relies on natural forces, such as wind and temperature differences, to move fresh air into a space and push stale air out. Unlike mechanical ventilation, it does not require any fans, ducts, or powered systems. Instead, it uses openings like windows, doors, vents, or specially designed architectural features to allow airflow. It is one of the simplest and most cost-effective ways to ventilate a building.

How Does Natural Ventilation Work

Natural ventilation works through two main principles:

a. Wind-Driven Ventilation: Wind naturally flows around and through buildings. When windows or vents are opened, the wind carries fresh air into the space and pushes stale air out. This works best in buildings designed to catch the wind, such as those with windows positioned on opposite sides of a room (cross-ventilation).

b. Buoyancy-Driven Ventilation (Stack Effect): Warm air is lighter than cool air and naturally rises. This creates a difference in pressure that allows hot air to escape through higher openings, like skylights or vents, while cooler, fresher air enters through lower openings, like ground-level windows or vents. This process is effective in taller buildings or during warm weather.

Features of Natural Ventilation

a. Openings for Airflow: Windows, doors, and vents are the primary features used to allow air to flow naturally into and out of a building.

b. Cross-Ventilation: Openings on opposite sides of a building create a pathway for air to move through, improving airflow and cooling efficiency.

c. Architectural Designs: Some buildings include features like atriums, courtyards, or louvers to maximize natural ventilation.

Advantages of Natural Ventilation

a. Energy Efficiency: Since no mechanical systems are involved, natural ventilation uses no electricity, making it highly energy-efficient and cost-saving.

b. Eco-Friendly: It reduces the need for energy consumption, which helps lower greenhouse gas emissions and promotes sustainability.

c. Low Maintenance: With no complex equipment involved, natural ventilation requires little to no maintenance, making it an affordable long-term option.

d. Improved Air Quality: Fresh outdoor air is introduced into the building, helping remove indoor pollutants, odors, and excess moisture.

e. Comfort: Natural airflow can create a comfortable environment, especially in mild climates or during cool evenings.

f. No Noise: Unlike mechanical systems, natural ventilation is completely silent.

Disadvantages of Natural Ventilation

a. Weather Dependent: The effectiveness of natural ventilation depends on weather conditions. It may not work well during extreme heat, cold, or when there is no wind.

b. Limited Control: Unlike mechanical systems, natural ventilation does not allow precise control over airflow or temperature.

c. Air Quality Concerns: If the outside air is polluted (e.g., from traffic, factories, or wildfires), bringing it inside could reduce indoor air quality.

d. Security Issues: Open windows and doors could pose a security risk, especially in urban or high-crime areas.

e. Inconsistent Ventilation: Airflow may be uneven, leaving some areas poorly ventilated while others receive too much air.

When to Use Natural Ventilation

Natural ventilation is ideal in the following situations:

i. Mild Climates: It works best in areas with moderate temperatures and low humidity.

ii. Low-Occupancy Spaces: Small homes, offices, or buildings with fewer occupants can benefit from natural ventilation.

iii. Good Outdoor Air Quality: It is suitable in locations where the outdoor air is clean and free of pollutants.

iv. Architecturally Designed Buildings: Buildings specifically designed for airflow can maximize the benefits of natural ventilation.

How to Enhance Natural Ventilation

a. Strategic Window Placement: Position windows and vents to promote cross-ventilation, allowing air to flow freely across rooms.

b. Use of Skylights and Chimneys: Install skylights, chimneys, or roof vents to encourage the stack effect, drawing warm air out and pulling cooler air in.

c. Airflow Barriers: Remove obstacles like large furniture that may block airflow.

d. Shading and Insulation: Combine natural ventilation with shading, to prevent excessive heat while keeping spaces comfortable.

e. Openings at Different Heights: Place vents or windows at both high and low points in a building to maximize airflow.

Natural ventilation is a simple and cost-effective way to improve indoor air quality and maintain comfort without relying on energy-intensive mechanical systems. While it has some limitations, such as dependence on weather conditions, it is a great option for homes and buildings in mild climates with good outdoor air quality. By designing spaces thoughtfully and optimizing airflow, natural ventilation can be an effective and sustainable ventilation solution in HVAC systems.

6.2 Mechanical Ventilation System

Mechanical ventilation is a type of ventilation system that uses powered devices, such as fans, blowers, and ductwork, to move air in and out of a building. Unlike natural ventilation, which relies on wind and temperature differences, mechanical ventilation provides a controlled and consistent way to ventilate indoor spaces, regardless of the weather or other external conditions. It is a key component of modern HVAC systems, ensuring fresh air circulation, removing stale air, and maintaining a healthy and comfortable indoor environment.

How Does Mechanical Ventilation Work

Mechanical ventilation systems use fans and ductwork to manage the flow of air. The system pulls fresh air from outside, filters it, and distributes it throughout the building. At the same time, stale or polluted air is extracted and vented outside. Advanced systems may include energy recovery components to make the process more efficient.

Types of Mechanical Ventilation Systems

a. Exhaust-Only Ventilation: This system uses exhaust fans to remove stale air from the building. Fresh air naturally enters the space through vents, cracks, or opening commonly used in bathrooms and kitchens to remove moisture, odors, and smoke.

b. Supply-Only Ventilation: A fan brings fresh outdoor air into the building and stale air exits naturally through cracks or exhaust vents. This method is ideal for areas where maintaining positive air pressure (to keep out pollutants or allergens) is important.

c. Balanced Ventilation: This system uses separate fans to bring in fresh air and exhaust stale air simultaneously. Balanced systems ensure even airflow and are ideal for maintaining indoor air quality in tightly sealed homes or buildings.

d. Energy Recovery Ventilation (ERV): ERV systems recover heat or energy from outgoing stale air and use it to pre-condition incoming fresh air. This makes the system more energy-efficient by reducing heating and cooling loads. Ideal for climates with extreme temperatures.

e. Heat Recovery Ventilation (HRV): Similar to ERV, but HRV systems focus solely on recovering heat from outgoing air to warm incoming air. Commonly used in colder climates to improve energy efficiency.

Components of Mechanical Ventilation Systems

i. Fans: Powered devices that move air in and out of the building.

ii. Ductwork: A network of pipes or channels that distributes air throughout the building.

iii. Air Filters: Filters remove dust, pollen, and other pollutants from incoming air, improving indoor air quality.

iv. Exhaust Vents: Openings that allow stale air to be vented outside.

v. Fresh Air Intakes: Openings where fresh outdoor air is drawn into the system.

vi. Energy or Heat Recovery Units (optional): Devices that improve efficiency by recovering heat or energy from outgoing air.

Advantages of Mechanical Ventilation

1. Consistent Airflow: Mechanical ventilation provides a steady and controlled flow of air, ensuring consistent ventilation at all times.

2. Improved Air Quality: Air filters remove pollutants, allergens, and harmful particles, delivering cleaner and healthier air indoors.

3. Moisture Control: Mechanical systems help regulate indoor humidity, reducing the risk of mold, mildew, and condensation.

4. Comfort: The system distributes air evenly, preventing stuffiness and maintaining a comfortable indoor environment.

5. Energy Efficiency: Advanced systems like ERV and HRV recover heat or energy, reducing heating and cooling costs.

6. Customizable: Mechanical systems can be designed to meet the specific needs of a building, such as ventilation for high-occupancy areas or spaces with specialized air quality requirements.

7. Weather Independence: Unlike natural ventilation, mechanical ventilation works effectively in all weather conditions.

Components Ventilation System

Fans, filters, and air ducts are essential components of ventilation systems. Together, they ensure proper air circulation, cleanliness, and distribution throughout a building. Here is a detailed look at each component and its role:

Fans

Fans are the driving force behind air movement in an HVAC system. They are responsible for pushing air through the ducts, delivering fresh air to different parts of the building, and removing stale air. Fans come in different types, such as exhaust fans, which remove air from specific areas like bathrooms and kitchens, and supply fans, which bring fresh air into the system. Larger systems may use blower fans, which are powerful and capable of moving large volumes of air.

Fans ensure that the air keeps flowing consistently and evenly throughout the building, maintaining comfort and air quality.

Filters

Filters are critical for cleaning the air that flows through the HVAC system. They trap dust, pollen, allergens, smoke, and other pollutants, preventing them from circulating in the indoor air. High-quality filters can even capture smaller particles, such as bacteria or mold spores, which improves indoor air quality and promotes health. Filters need to be cleaned or replaced regularly to ensure they work efficiently. Dirty or clogged filters can restrict airflow, making the system work harder, which reduces energy efficiency and can lead to higher utility bills or system damage.

Air   Ducts

Air ducts are the pathways that carry air throughout the building. They distribute fresh air from the HVAC system to different rooms and return stale air to the system for filtering or exhausting. Ducts are usually made of metal, plastic, or fiberglass and are insulated to maintain the desired air temperature during distribution. Properly designed and sealed air ducts are important to prevent air leaks, which can waste energy and reduce the system's effectiveness. Regular maintenance and cleaning of ducts are necessary to prevent the buildup of dust and debris, which can affect airflow and indoor air quality.

Together, fans, filters, and air ducts ensure that air is effectively moved, cleaned, and delivered throughout the building, contributing to a healthy and comfortable indoor environment. These components work as a team to support the HVAC system's primary goal of maintaining proper ventilation and air quality.

Chapter Seven: Indoor Air Quality (IAQ)

Indoor Air Quality (IAQ) refers to the quality of the air inside buildings and how it affects the health and comfort of occupants. HVAC systems play a key role in maintaining good IAQ by regulating temperature, humidity, and ventilation. They filter out pollutants, allergens, and other harmful particles, while also ensuring proper airflow to prevent stale air and excessive moisture. A well-maintained HVAC system can help create a healthier indoor environment by reducing the risk of respiratory issues, odors, and mold growth.

7.1 Understanding Pollutants and Allergens

Pollutants and allergens are particles, chemicals, or biological substances in the air that can negatively impact indoor air quality (IAQ) and cause health problems. The HVAC system plays a key role in managing these contaminants to create a cleaner and healthier indoor environment. Let's understand what pollutants and allergens are, where they come from, and how HVAC systems help deal with them.

What Are Pollutants and Allergens

1. Pollutants: Pollutants are unwanted substances in the air that can harm health or cause discomfort. They include:

a. Dust and Dirt: Tiny particles that settle on surfaces and float in the air.

b. Smoke: From tobacco, cooking, or burning materials, which releases harmful chemicals.

c. Chemical Vapors: Emitted by cleaning products, paints, adhesives, and building materials, such as volatile organic compounds (VOCs).

d. Carbon Monoxide (CO): A harmful gas that can come from gas stoves, heaters, or vehicles.

e. Mold Spores: Released by mold growing in damp or poorly ventilated areas.

f. Pollen: From plants, this can enter the home through open doors, windows, or on clothing.

2. Allergens: Allergens are substances that can trigger allergic reactions in sensitive individuals. Common allergens include:

a. Pet Dander: Small flakes of skin shed by cats, dogs, and other pets.

b. Dust Mites: Tiny insects that thrive in carpets, bedding, and upholstery.

c. Mold Spores: A type of allergen that can cause respiratory issues.

d. Pollen: Especially problematic during certain seasons when plants release it into the air.

Where Do They Come From

a. Indoor Sources: Dust, smoke from cooking or candles, pet dander, and chemicals from household products.

b. Outdoor Sources: Pollutants like car exhaust, industrial emissions, and pollen can enter through open windows, doors, or ventilation systems.

c. Moisture Problems: High humidity or water leaks can lead to mold growth, which releases spores into the air.

How Do Pollutants and Allergens Affect Health

Pollutants and allergens can cause a range of health problems, including:

a. Respiratory issues, such as asthma or bronchitis.

b. Allergic reactions, like sneezing, runny nose, or itchy eyes.

c. Fatigue or headaches due to exposure to chemical pollutants like VOCs or carbon monoxide.

d. Long-term exposure to certain pollutants, like tobacco smoke or industrial chemicals, can lead to serious conditions, including heart or lung disease.

How HVAC Systems Help Manage Pollutants and Allergens

a. Air Filters: HVAC systems use filters to trap dust, pollen, pet dander, and other particles. High-efficiency filters, such as HEPA filters, can capture even smaller particles, improving indoor air quality significantly.
b. Ventilation: HVAC systems ensure proper ventilation by bringing in fresh outdoor air and expelling stale indoor air. This helps dilute pollutants and reduce their concentration indoors.
c. Humidity Control: By regulating indoor humidity levels, HVAC systems prevent the growth of mold and dust mites, which thrive in damp environments.
d. Air Purifiers: Some HVAC systems include built-in air purifiers or can be paired with standalone units to remove airborne allergens and pollutants more effectively.
e. Duct Maintenance: Clean ducts are essential to prevent the accumulation and circulation of dust, mold, and other contaminants. Regular duct cleaning keeps pollutants from spreading throughout the building.
f. Carbon Monoxide Detectors: Modern HVAC systems often include safety features like carbon monoxide detectors to monitor and alert occupants of dangerous gas levels.

Maintaining an HVAC System to Combat Pollutants and Allergens

To ensure your HVAC system works effectively in managing pollutants and allergens:
i. Replace air filters regularly, at least every 1–3 months, or as recommended by the manufacturer.

ii. Schedule routine HVAC maintenance to check for any issues that may affect air quality.

iii. Keep air ducts clean and sealed to prevent the buildup and circulation of pollutants.

iv. Use ventilation systems properly by opening vents and avoiding blockages.

v. Control humidity levels by using a dehumidifier if necessary, especially in humid climates.

Pollutants and allergens are common contributors to poor indoor air quality, but a well-maintained HVAC system can significantly reduce their presence. By filtering air, improving ventilation, controlling humidity, and incorporating air purification, HVAC systems help create a healthier, more comfortable indoor environment. Understanding the sources and impacts of these contaminants makes it easier to take the right steps to keep indoor air clean and safe for everyone.

7.2 Ventilation Strategies for Cleaner Air

Ventilation strategies are methods used in HVAC systems to improve indoor air quality by bringing in fresh outdoor air, removing stale indoor air, and filtering out pollutants. Proper ventilation is essential for creating a healthy and comfortable indoor environment. Here are some effective strategies used in HVAC systems to achieve cleaner air:

1. Natural Ventilation: This strategy relies on natural forces, like wind and temperature differences, to move fresh air into a building and push stale air out. Open windows, doors, and vents are common ways to allow air to circulate naturally. While simple and energy-efficient, natural ventilation depends on outdoor conditions and may not always be effective in maintaining consistent air quality, especially in extreme weather or highly polluted areas.

2. Mechanical Ventilation: Mechanical ventilation uses fans, blowers, and ductwork to control airflow. Fresh air is drawn into the building while stale air is removed. This strategy allows for consistent ventilation, regardless of outdoor conditions. It is commonly used in residential, commercial, and industrial HVAC systems. Mechanical ventilation systems can also include air filters to remove pollutants and allergens.

3. Exhaust Ventilation: Exhaust fans are installed to remove specific types of air pollutants or moisture from areas like kitchens and bathrooms. These fans expel stale air directly to the outside, helping to reduce odors, smoke, and humidity. This is especially useful in areas prone to mold growth or poor air circulation.

4. Supply Ventilation: In this strategy, fresh outdoor air is introduced into the building using a fan, and the stale indoor air exits naturally through cracks, vents, or exhaust systems. Supply ventilation is particularly effective in maintaining positive air pressure, which can keep outdoor pollutants like dust and pollen from entering the building.

5. Balanced Ventilation: Balanced ventilation systems use separate fans to bring in fresh air and remove stale air simultaneously. This ensures an even exchange of air, maintaining good air

quality throughout the building. These systems are ideal for tightly sealed homes or buildings where air circulation is limited.

6. Energy Recovery Ventilation (ERV) Systems: ERV systems improve ventilation efficiency by transferring heat and moisture between incoming and outgoing air. This reduces energy costs while maintaining comfort. For example, in winter, warm indoor air preheats the incoming cold air, and in summer, cooler indoor air preconditions the incoming warm air.

7. Heat Recovery Ventilation (HRV) Systems: Similar to ERV systems, HRV systems focus on transferring heat between incoming and outgoing air, without transferring moisture. These are particularly useful in colder climates to retain indoor warmth while ensuring proper ventilation.

8. Advanced Air Filtration and Purification: Many HVAC systems incorporate air filters or purifiers to clean incoming air. High-efficiency filters, such as HEPA filters, can capture small particles like pollen, dust, and smoke, while advanced purification systems, like UV lights or ionizers, can remove bacteria, viruses, and odors.

9. Zoned Ventilation: This strategy divides a building into zones, each with its own ventilation requirements. For example, areas with higher occupancy or more pollutants, like kitchens or conference rooms, may receive more ventilation than less-used spaces. Zoned ventilation ensures that air quality is tailored to the specific needs of different areas.

10. Humidity Control: Proper ventilation strategies often include humidity management to maintain comfortable and healthy indoor air. High humidity levels can lead to mold growth, while low humidity can cause dryness and discomfort. Dehumidifiers or humidifiers can be integrated into the HVAC system to keep humidity levels in the optimal range of 30–50%.

11. Smart Ventilation Systems: Modern HVAC systems can include smart ventilation technology, which uses sensors and automation to adjust ventilation based on real-time conditions.

12. Regular Maintenance and Cleaning: For any ventilation strategy to be effective, regular maintenance is crucial. This includes cleaning air ducts, replacing filters, checking fans and vents, and ensuring all components are working correctly. A well-maintained HVAC system operates more efficiently and provides cleaner air.

By using these ventilation strategies, HVAC systems can significantly improve indoor air quality, reduce the presence of pollutants and allergens, and create a healthier, more comfortable living or working environment.

7. 3 Balancing Ventilation

Balancing ventilation with energy efficiency in HVAC systems is essential to create a healthy indoor environment while minimizing energy costs. Ventilation ensures fresh air enters the building and stale air is removed, but if not done efficiently, it can lead to energy waste, especially in heating or cooling seasons. Here is how HVAC systems manage this balance:

First, energy recovery systems like Heat Recovery Ventilators (HRVs) or Energy Recovery Ventilators (ERVs) are used. These systems transfer heat or energy between outgoing stale air and incoming fresh air. For example, in winter, the warmth from the outgoing air preheats the fresh, cold air entering the building. In summer, cooler outgoing air helps precondition warm incoming air. This process reduces the workload on heating or cooling systems and saves energy.

Proper sealing and insulation of the building also play a critical role. Air leaks around windows, doors, and ducts can lead to energy loss when ventilation systems are running. Sealing these leaks ensures that the fresh air brought in by the HVAC system is used efficiently without escaping the building.

Using demand-controlled ventilation is another way to maintain efficiency. This involves adjusting ventilation based on occupancy or air quality needs. For instance, sensors can detect when a room is empty and reduce ventilation to save energy. Conversely, when a room is crowded, the system increases airflow to maintain good air quality.

High-efficiency fans and motors are often used in modern HVAC systems. These components use less electricity while still providing adequate airflow, which reduces energy consumption.

Zoning is another effective method. This divides the building into different areas, each with its own ventilation and temperature controls. By ventilating only the occupied zones, energy use is minimized.

Advanced air filters also help in balancing ventilation with energy efficiency. Clean air filters allow air to flow easily through the system, reducing the energy required to push air through. Regularly replacing or cleaning filters ensures that the system operates efficiently.

Smart HVAC systems further improve the balance by using automation and real-time data. These systems can adjust ventilation and temperature settings based on outdoor weather, indoor air quality, and energy demand. For instance, if outdoor conditions are mild, the system might reduce mechanical ventilation and rely more on natural ventilation to save energy.

Finally, regular maintenance of the HVAC system is critical. A well-maintained system runs more efficiently, ensuring that ventilation does not lead to unnecessary energy consumption. This includes cleaning ducts, checking seals, and ensuring all components are working properly.

In summary, balancing ventilation with energy efficiency involves using energy recovery systems, sealing air leaks, employing demand-controlled ventilation, using efficient components, and incorporating smart technology. These strategies ensure good air quality while keeping energy usage and costs under control.

Part Four: Air Conditioning Systems

Chapter Eight: Overview of Air Conditioning

Air conditioning is the process of cooling and dehumidifying indoor air to create a comfortable environment. It is an essential part of HVAC systems, especially in hot and humid climates. Air conditioners work by removing heat from the air inside a building and releasing it outside, using components like compressors, refrigerants, evaporator coils, and condenser coils. They also help control humidity levels, improve air circulation, and filter out dust and allergens. Air conditioning is widely used in homes, offices, and commercial spaces to maintain a pleasant and healthy indoor atmosphere.

Types of Air Conditioning Systems

1. Window Units Air Conditioning

Window units are a popular and affordable type of air conditioning system that is designed to cool a single room or a small space. They are compact, self-contained units that fit into a window frame or a specially designed wall opening. Window air conditioners are widely used in homes, apartments, and offices where central air conditioning may not be available or practical.

How Do Window Units Work

Window air conditioners work by using a refrigeration cycle to remove heat and humidity from the indoor air and release it outside. The unit has two main sides:

a. Indoor Side: This part faces the inside of the room and contains the evaporator coil and fan. The evaporator coil absorbs heat from the indoor air, and the fan blows the cooled air back into the room.

b. Outdoor Side: This part faces outside the building and contains the condenser coil and compressor. The condenser coil releases the absorbed heat to the outdoor air, while the compressor circulates the refrigerant needed for the cooling process.

Advantages of Window Units

a. Cost-Effective: Window units are one of the most affordable air conditioning options, both in terms of initial purchase and installation.

b. Easy Installation: These units are relatively easy to install and do not require extensive ductwork or professional expertise. Many people can install them on their own with basic tools.

c. Compact Design: Window air conditioners are compact and do not take up floor space, making them ideal for small rooms or spaces with limited space.

d. Portability: While not as portable as portable AC units, window units can be easily moved from one window to another if needed.

e. Energy Efficiency for Small Spaces: For cooling a single room, window units are often more energy-efficient than running a central HVAC system.

Limitations of Window Units

a. Limited Coverage: Window units are designed to cool only one room or a small space, so they are not suitable for large areas or whole-house cooling.

b. Window Availability: A window or wall opening is required for installation, which might not always be possible or convenient in some spaces.

c. Noise Levels: Compared to central air conditioning systems, window units can be noisy because all the components are contained in a single box.

d. Aesthetic Concerns: The unit can obstruct the window and impact the exterior appearance of the building.

e. Energy Usage: While efficient for small spaces, using multiple window units for several rooms can be less energy-efficient than a central air system.

Maintenance of Window Units.

Proper maintenance ensures the efficiency and longevity of a window air conditioner:

a. Clean or Replace Filters: Filters should be cleaned or replaced regularly to maintain good airflow and air quality.

b. Check the Coils: The evaporator and condenser coils should be cleaned periodically to prevent dust buildup.

c. Inspect the Seals: Ensure the seal around the unit and the window is tight to prevent air leaks.

d. Drainage: Check the drainage system to ensure that condensation is properly expelled from the unit.

Window air conditioners are a convenient and cost-effective solution for cooling individual rooms or small spaces. They are simple to install and operate, making them a popular choice for homes and apartments. However, they are best suited for single-room use and may not be ideal for larger spaces or households that require whole-house cooling.

2. Split Systems Air Conditioning

Split systems are a common type of air conditioning system used to cool and heat indoor spaces. They are called "split" because the system is divided into two main parts: an indoor unit and an outdoor unit. These systems are popular for both residential and commercial use due to their efficiency, quiet operation, and ability to cool larger spaces compared to window units.

How Do Split Systems Work.

Split systems operate using a refrigeration cycle, similar to other types of air conditioners. The indoor unit contains the evaporator coil, which absorbs heat from the indoor air, and a fan that circulates the cooled air back into the room. The outdoor unit houses the condenser coil and compressor, which release the absorbed heat into the outdoor air.

The two units are connected by copper refrigerant lines that allow the refrigerant to flow between them, facilitating the cooling process. The refrigerant absorbs heat from the indoor air inside the evaporator coil, and then, in the outdoor unit, the refrigerant releases this heat through the condenser coil.

Key Components of a Split System

i. Indoor Unit: The indoor unit is installed inside the building, often mounted on a wall or ceiling. It houses the evaporator coil, fan, and air filter. This unit pulls warm air from the room, cools it, and then blows the cooled air back into the room.

ii. Outdoor Unit: The outdoor unit is placed outside the building, often on the ground or mounted on a wall. It contains the compressor and condenser coil. The compressor pumps refrigerant through the system, and the condenser coil expels the heat absorbed by the refrigerant to the outdoor air.

Advantages of Split Systems

a. Quiet Operation: Because the noisy components, such as the compressor and condenser coil, are located outside the building, split systems operate more quietly than window units or portable air conditioners.

b. Efficient Cooling and Heating: Split systems are efficient at cooling or heating large spaces and can be used for both purposes in many cases, especially with systems that include a heat pump function.

c. Zoning Capability: Some split systems come with multiple indoor units connected to a single outdoor unit, allowing for zoned cooling and heating. This means you can control the temperature in different rooms or areas of the building independently.

d. Space-Saving: Split systems do not require bulky equipment to be placed inside the living space, as the indoor unit is compact and can be mounted on a wall or ceiling, saving floor space.

e. Energy Efficiency: Split systems tend to be more energy-efficient than window units and can provide better comfort for larger areas with lower energy consumption, especially when combined with programmable thermostats or variable-speed fans.

Limitations of Split Systems

a. Installation Complexity: Installing a split system requires professional help, as it involves running refrigerant lines between the indoor and outdoor units. This can make installation more expensive and time-consuming compared to window units or portable air conditioners.

b. Higher Initial Cost: While the operating costs of a split system may be lower than other options, the initial cost of the system, including installation, can be higher than simpler systems like window units.

c. Outdoor Unit Space: The outdoor unit needs to be installed outside the building, which requires space and may affect the aesthetic of the home or building.

d. Maintenance: Split systems require regular maintenance, such as cleaning or replacing filters, inspecting refrigerant levels, and checking for any issues with the coils or compressor. Neglecting maintenance can reduce efficiency and shorten the system's lifespan.

Maintenance of Split Systems.

To keep a split system running efficiently, regular maintenance is necessary:

a. Clean or Replace Filters: Air filters should be cleaned or replaced regularly to prevent clogging and maintain airflow.

b. Inspect Refrigerant Levels: Refrigerant should be checked to ensure there are no leaks or low levels, as low refrigerant can cause the system to lose efficiency.

c. Clean Coils: The evaporator and condenser coils should be cleaned periodically to prevent dirt buildup, which can hinder the system's performance.

d. Check the Outdoor Unit: The outdoor unit should be kept clear of debris, like leaves or dirt, to ensure proper airflow and function.

3. Packaged Units Air Conditioning

Packaged units are another type of air conditioning system commonly used for cooling and heating large spaces. Unlike split systems, which have separate indoor and outdoor units, a packaged unit combines all the components of the system into one single unit. This makes them a convenient and space-saving option for both residential and commercial applications.

How Do Packaged Units Work.

A packaged unit operates similarly to other air conditioners, using a refrigeration cycle to cool the indoor air. However, unlike split systems, all the components—such as the compressor, condenser, evaporator coil, and fan—are housed in a single, self-contained unit. This unit is typically placed outside the building, either on the roof or the ground, and it works by drawing in warm air, cooling it, and then distributing the cooled air through ducts to the indoor spaces.

The compressor inside the packaged unit circulates refrigerant through the system. The refrigerant absorbs heat from the indoor air and carries it to the outdoor unit, where the heat is released into the surrounding environment. This process cools the indoor air and helps to control humidity.

Key Components of Packaged Units

a. Compressor: The compressor is responsible for circulating refrigerant throughout the system. It compresses the refrigerant, turning it into a high-pressure gas that moves through the coils and releases heat outside.

b. Condenser Coil: The condenser coil releases the heat absorbed by the refrigerant to the outside air. It is located in the outdoor portion of the unit.

c. Evaporator Coil: The evaporator coil is responsible for absorbing heat from the indoor air. It is typically located inside the packaged unit, where the cool air is blown through the system to be distributed throughout the building.

d. Blower/Fan: The blower fan circulates air through the evaporator coil and into the ductwork, helping to distribute the cooled air evenly throughout the indoor spaces.

Advantages of Packaged Units

e. Space-Saving: Since all the components are housed in one unit, packaged units do not require additional indoor space for the air handling unit. This makes them ideal for buildings with limited indoor space or where ceiling-mounted systems are not practical.

f. Easier Installation: The installation process is typically easier and faster because there is only one unit to install, and it can be placed outside the building. This also eliminates the need to run refrigerant lines between the indoor and outdoor units, as is required with split systems.

g. Suitable for Large Spaces: Packaged units are commonly used in commercial buildings, large homes, and industrial applications because they are capable of cooling and heating large areas effectively.

h. Improved Aesthetics: Because the unit is placed outside the building, it does not take up valuable indoor space or impact the interior décor.

i. Integrated Heating and Cooling: Many packaged units offer both heating and cooling capabilities, making them versatile systems that can be used year-round. Some packaged units include heat pumps or gas/electric heating options.

Limitations of Packaged Units

a. Outdoor Placement: Since the entire system is contained in one unit, it needs to be placed outdoors. This means you need enough space outside to install the unit, which can be a challenge in smaller or densely populated areas.

b. Noise: While packaged units are typically quieter than window units, the compressor and fan can still produce some noise when operating. Depending on where the unit is installed, this may be noticeable to people nearby.

c. Maintenance: As with all HVAC systems, regular maintenance is important. Cleaning filters, checking refrigerant levels, and ensuring the coils are functioning properly are all necessary to keep the system running efficiently.

d. Higher Upfront Cost: The initial cost of a packaged unit can be higher than a window unit or smaller HVAC systems, though it may still be more affordable than installing a full central air system.

Maintenance of Packaged Units.

Proper maintenance ensures the longevity and efficiency of the packaged unit:

a. Clean or Replace Filters: Clean or replace filters regularly to ensure proper airflow and maintain air quality.

b. Check Refrigerant Levels: Ensure that the refrigerant is at the right levels to prevent the system from running inefficiently or damaging components.

c. Clean the Coils: Clean both the evaporator and condenser coils to remove dirt and debris, which can reduce system efficiency.

d. Inspect the Blower: Check the blower and fan for wear and tear to ensure they are operating effectively and distributing air properly.

e. Inspect for Leaks: Check the unit for any refrigerant or air leaks that could affect the performance of the system.

4. Central Air Conditioning

Central air conditioning is one of the most common and effective cooling solutions used in homes, offices, and larger buildings. Unlike window units or split systems, which cool individual rooms, central air conditioning systems cool an entire building or multiple rooms at once, providing consistent comfort throughout the space.

How Does Central Air Conditioning Work.

Central air conditioning operates through a network of ducts and vents that circulate cool air throughout the building. It consists of two main parts: the indoor unit (also called the air handler) and the outdoor unit (also called the condenser).

i. Indoor Unit: The indoor unit contains the evaporator coil and blower fan. The system pulls warm air from inside the building through return air ducts. The air is then passed over the evaporator coil, where it is cooled by the refrigerant inside the coil. Once cooled, the air is blown back into the rooms through supply ducts and vents.

ii. Outdoor Unit: The outdoor unit contains the compressor and condenser coil. The compressor pumps refrigerant through the system. The refrigerant absorbs heat from the indoor air at the evaporator coil and moves to the condenser coil outside, where it releases the absorbed heat into the outside air.

Key Components of Central Air Conditioning

a. Evaporator Coil: Located inside the air handler, this coil absorbs heat from the indoor air and cools it.

b. Condenser Coil: Located in the outdoor unit, the condenser coil releases the absorbed heat from the refrigerant to the outside air.

c. Compressor: The compressor pumps refrigerant through the system, circulating it between the evaporator and condenser coils.

d. Blower Fan: The fan in the indoor unit blows cooled air through the ducts and into the building.

e. Thermostat: The thermostat controls the temperature inside the building. It tells the system when to turn on and off based on the desired temperature.

Advantages of Central Air Conditioning

a. Whole-House Cooling: Central air conditioning can cool an entire house or building evenly, making it ideal for larger spaces. Unlike window units, which only cool one room, central AC ensures that all rooms are comfortable at the same time.

b. Quiet Operation: Because the noisy components (such as the compressor) are located outside the building, central air conditioning operates much more quietly than window or portable air conditioners.

c. Improved Air Quality: Central AC systems often include air filters that help remove dust, allergens, and other particles from the air, improving indoor air quality. Some systems also include humidifiers or dehumidifiers to control indoor moisture levels.

d. Aesthetic Appeal: Central air conditioning systems are hidden from view. The indoor unit is typically installed in a closet, attic, or basement, and only the vents in the walls or ceilings are visible. This makes them a more aesthetically pleasing option for homeowners.

e. Energy Efficiency: For cooling larger homes, central air conditioning is generally more energy-efficient than using multiple window units or portable air conditioners. It is also more cost-effective in the long run, especially when properly maintained.

Limitations of Central Air Conditioning

a. High Initial Cost: The installation of a central air conditioning system can be more expensive than smaller cooling systems like window units. This is due to the need for ductwork and professional installation.

b. Installation Complexity: Installing central air conditioning requires careful planning and professional expertise, especially if the home or building does not already have ductwork in place.

c. Ongoing Maintenance: Central air conditioning systems require regular maintenance, including cleaning or replacing filters, checking refrigerant levels, and ensuring the ducts are clear of dust and debris. Failure to maintain the system can reduce its efficiency and lifespan.

d. Energy Consumption: While central air conditioning is generally more energy-efficient than using multiple window units, it can still consume a lot of energy, especially in large homes. Using a programmable thermostat can help reduce energy use by automatically adjusting the temperature when the building is unoccupied.

Maintenance of Central Air Conditioning.

To ensure a long lifespan and efficient operation, regular maintenance is necessary:

a. Clean or Replace Filters: Air filters should be cleaned or replaced every few months to maintain good airflow and air quality.

b. Inspect Refrigerant Levels: Low refrigerant levels can cause the system to overheat and decrease its cooling ability. Regular checks are important.

c. Check the Ductwork: Make sure the ducts are clear of dust, debris, and blockages that could prevent proper airflow.

d. Clean the Coils: Both the evaporator and condenser coils should be cleaned periodically to remove dirt that can reduce efficiency.

e. Inspect the Thermostat: Ensure that the thermostat is calibrated correctly to avoid inconsistent cooling.

Central air conditioning is a great choice for cooling larger homes or buildings. It provides consistent, whole-house comfort with quiet operation and improved air quality. Although the initial cost of installation can be higher and the system requires regular maintenance, the benefits of energy efficiency, convenience, and comfort make it a worthwhile investment for many households and businesses. Regular upkeep and professional service will ensure that the system runs efficiently and provides long-lasting comfort for years.

5. Mini-Split Air Conditioning System

Mini-split systems are a type of air conditioning system that is commonly used to cool or heat individual rooms or smaller spaces. They are similar to split systems, but with a more compact design and the ability to control the temperature in different areas (or "zones") of a home or building. Mini-split systems are a great choice for homes or spaces where traditional ductwork is not feasible, or where there is a need for zone-based temperature control.

How Do Mini-Split Systems Work

A mini-split system operates in a similar way to a split system air conditioner, but with a key difference: instead of a single indoor unit, mini-split systems can have multiple indoor units connected to one outdoor unit. Each indoor unit can be controlled individually, allowing you to set different temperatures in different rooms or areas.

The system uses a refrigeration cycle to cool or heat the indoor air. The outdoor unit houses the compressor and condenser coil, while the indoor unit contains the evaporator coil and a fan. The refrigerant circulates between the indoor and outdoor units, absorbing heat from the indoor air and releasing it outside (for cooling) or absorbing heat from outside and bringing it inside (for heating, if the system includes a heat pump).

Key Components of Mini-Split Systems

a. Outdoor Unit: The outdoor unit contains the compressor, condenser coil, and expansion valve. It is responsible for circulating refrigerant through the system and releasing absorbed heat into the outside air (during cooling) or absorbing heat from the outdoor air (during heating).

b. Indoor Unit: The indoor unit houses the evaporator coil and fan. It cools or heats the air inside the room by blowing air over the evaporator coil. Mini-split systems can have multiple indoor units connected to one outdoor unit, allowing for different temperature settings in each room or zone.

c. Refrigerant Lines: Copper refrigerant lines connect the indoor and outdoor units, allowing the refrigerant to circulate between them and facilitate the cooling or heating process.

d. Remote Control or Thermostat: Mini-split systems usually come with a remote control that allows users to adjust the temperature and settings for each indoor unit. Some models may also use a central thermostat for managing temperature in all zones.

Advantages of Mini-Split Systems

a. Zoned Cooling and Heating: One of the key advantages of mini-split systems is their ability to provide zoned cooling and heating. Each indoor unit can be set to a different temperature, allowing for personalized comfort in different rooms or areas of the building.

b. No Ductwork Required: Mini-split systems are ductless, meaning they don't require the installation of traditional ductwork, which can be expensive and difficult to retrofit in older homes. This makes mini-split systems ideal for retrofitting or adding air conditioning in homes without existing ducts.

c. Energy Efficiency: Mini-split systems are generally more energy-efficient than window units or portable air conditioners because they only cool or heat the specific areas that need it. They avoid the energy losses associated with ducted systems. Many mini-split systems also come with energy-saving features, such as inverter technology, which adjusts the compressor speed based on the cooling or heating demand.

d. Quiet Operation: Mini-split systems are known for their quiet operation. The noisy components, such as the compressor and condenser, are located in the outdoor unit, leaving the indoor units to operate quietly.

e. Space-Saving Design: Mini-split systems are compact and can be mounted on walls or ceilings, saving floor space. They are less intrusive and can blend well with a variety of home décor styles.

Limitations of Mini-Split Systems

a. Higher Upfront Cost: The initial installation cost of a mini-split system is higher than that of window units or portable air conditioners. However, this cost can be offset by the system's energy efficiency and long-term savings.

b. Professional Installation Required: Installing a mini-split system requires professional installation. The system involves running refrigerant lines and mounting the indoor units, which requires expertise to ensure proper function and efficiency.

c. Maintenance Needs: Like any HVAC system, mini-split systems require regular maintenance. Cleaning filters, checking refrigerant levels, and ensuring the system is operating properly are important tasks that should be performed regularly.

d. Aesthetic Impact: While mini-split systems are compact, the indoor units are still visible. Some homeowners may find the appearance of the wall-mounted units less aesthetically pleasing than hidden ductwork. However, there are options to install the indoor units in less noticeable places, such as high on walls or in the ceiling.

Maintenance of Mini-Split Systems

Regular maintenance is important to keep a mini-split system running smoothly and efficiently:

a. Clean or Replace Filters: Clean or replace the air filters regularly to maintain good airflow and indoor air quality.

b. Check Refrigerant Levels: Ensure that refrigerant levels are adequate to prevent inefficient cooling or heating.

c. Clean the Coils: Clean the evaporator and condenser coils to remove dirt and debris, which can decrease the system's efficiency.

d. Inspect the Ductless Lines: Check for any leaks or blockages in the refrigerant lines to ensure the system is functioning properly.

Mini-split systems are an excellent choice for those who want efficient, zoned cooling and heating without the need for ductwork. These systems provide flexibility, comfort, and energy savings, making them ideal for homes, apartments, and buildings that do not have existing ducts or where installing ducts would be difficult or expensive. With proper maintenance, mini-split systems can provide long-lasting comfort and efficient climate control, while allowing for customized temperatures in different rooms or areas.

Chapter Nine: How Air Conditioning Works; The Refrigeration Cycle

Air conditioning systems are designed to cool indoor spaces by removing heat from the air. They achieve this by using a process called the refrigeration cycle. The refrigeration cycle is a continuous loop in which refrigerant (a special fluid) absorbs heat from the indoor air and releases it outside, effectively cooling the indoor environment. This process involves several key steps, which work together to move heat from inside to outside.

Here is a step-by-step breakdown of how the refrigeration cycle works in an air conditioning system:

1. The Compressor (Outdoor Unit): The refrigeration cycle starts in the outdoor unit, where the compressor is located. The compressor takes the refrigerant gas that has already absorbed heat from the indoor air and compresses it, turning it into a high-pressure, high-temperature gas. This process increases the pressure and energy of the refrigerant, preparing it to release the heat it has collected.

2. The Condenser Coil (Outdoor Unit): Once the refrigerant gas is compressed, it flows into the condenser coil in the outdoor unit. As the hot refrigerant gas passes through the condenser coil, the outdoor air (blown by the fan in the outdoor unit) cools it down. The refrigerant gas condenses into a liquid state because it is releasing the heat it absorbed from the indoor air. This is why the condenser coil feels warm to the touch—it's where the heat is transferred from the refrigerant into the outside air.

3. The Expansion Valve (Indoor Unit): After the refrigerant has been cooled and condensed into a high-pressure liquid, it moves toward the indoor unit and passes through the expansion valve. The expansion valve controls the flow of refrigerant into the evaporator coil. As the refrigerant passes through this valve, its pressure drops, and it begins to expand and cool rapidly. The expansion valve is key in turning the refrigerant into a cool, low-pressure liquid.

4. The Evaporator Coil (Indoor Unit): The next step occurs in the evaporator coil, located in the indoor unit of the air conditioning system. As the cold refrigerant moves through the evaporator coil, it absorbs heat from the indoor air. A fan inside the indoor unit blows warm indoor air over the evaporator coil. As the air passes over the coil, the refrigerant absorbs the heat from the air, and the air cools down. The cool air is then blown back into the room, lowering the temperature of the space. The refrigerant, now warmed by the heat it has absorbed from the indoor air, changes from a low-pressure liquid back into a gas. This process of heat absorption from the air helps cool the room effectively.

5. The Refrigerant Returns to the Compressor: After the refrigerant passes through the evaporator coil, it is a low-pressure gas again. This gas returns to the compressor, where the cycle begins all over again. The compressor will compress the gas, sending it back through the condenser coil to release the heat it has absorbed, and the cycle continues.

The Key Steps in the Refrigeration Cycle

a. The compressor compresses the refrigerant, turning it into a high-pressure gas.

b. The condenser coil releases heat from the refrigerant to the outside air, turning it into a high-pressure liquid.

c. The expansion valve reduces the refrigerant's pressure, causing it to cool and expand into a low-pressure liquid.

d. The evaporator coil absorbs heat from the indoor air, turning the refrigerant into a gas and cooling the air.

e. The refrigerant returns to the compressor to start the cycle again.

Why Is the Refrigeration Cycle Important in Air Conditioning. The refrigeration cycle is at the heart of every air conditioning system. It allows the system to continuously cool the indoor air by transferring heat from inside the building to the outside. This process works efficiently and effectively, providing the comfort of a cool indoor environment even when the outside temperature is hot.

By using this cycle, air conditioners can lower the temperature in a space without creating additional heat. Instead, they simply move heat from one place (inside the room) to another (outside the building), which is why air conditioning is such an effective way to maintain a comfortable indoor climate.

Understanding the refrigeration cycle helps explain how air conditioning systems maintain efficiency and why regular maintenance, such as checking refrigerant levels and cleaning coils, is so important to keep the system running smoothly.

Factors to Consider When Choosing an Air Conditioning System

Choosing the right air conditioning (AC) system for your home or building is an important decision that can impact your comfort, energy efficiency, and overall costs. With so many types of air conditioning systems available, it can be challenging to determine which one is the best fit for your needs. Here are the key factors to consider when choosing an air conditioning system:

1. Size and Cooling Capacity: One of the most important factors to consider is the size of the AC system and its cooling capacity. The cooling capacity is measured in BTUs (British Thermal Units), which indicates how much heat the system can remove from a space per hour. An undersized AC system will struggle to cool the area effectively, while an oversized system may lead to higher energy bills and inefficient operation.

To determine the right size, you need to consider:

i. The square footage of the space you want to cool

ii. The number of windows and doors in the room

iii. The amount of sunlight the room receives

iv. The insulation and air tightness of the room

A professional HVAC technician can perform a load calculation to ensure the system is properly sized for your space.

2. Energy Efficiency: Energy efficiency is another crucial factor when choosing an AC system. An energy-efficient unit uses less electricity to cool your space, which can help lower your utility bills and reduce your environmental impact. Look for an air conditioning system with a high SEER (Seasonal Energy Efficiency Ratio) rating. The higher the SEER rating, the more energy-efficient the system is. Modern systems, especially those with inverter technology, are designed to adjust their compressor speed based on the cooling demand. This can further improve energy efficiency compared to older models.

3. The Type of Air Conditioning System: There are different types of air conditioning systems, each suited to different needs and spaces. The main types include:

i. Window Units: These are small, affordable units that fit in a window and cool one room at a time. They are easy to install but may not be effective for larger spaces.

ii. Split Systems: These systems consist of an indoor unit and an outdoor unit, providing more efficient cooling than window units. They can cool multiple rooms and are quieter, but they require professional installation.

iii. Mini-Split Systems: These are similar to split systems but do not require ductwork. They are ideal for smaller spaces or homes without existing ducts and offer the flexibility of zone-based cooling.

iv. Packaged Systems: In these systems, all components are housed in a single unit, typically installed outside. They are suitable for homes or buildings without the space for separate indoor and outdoor units.

v. Central Air Conditioning: This system is designed to cool an entire home or building using ducts. It's ideal for large homes with multiple rooms, but it requires significant installation and regular maintenance.

Consider the space you need to cool and whether you need a whole-house solution or just need to cool specific rooms.

4. Installation and Maintenance Costs: The installation cost can vary depending on the type of system, the complexity of the installation, and the need for any additional modifications (such as ductwork or electrical work). Window units and portable air conditioners tend to have lower installation costs, while systems like central air or mini-split systems may require more significant upfront investment. It is also important to think about long-term maintenance. Some systems, like central air conditioning, require regular maintenance of ducts, filters, and coils. Mini-split systems, on the other hand, may require less maintenance, though the filters still need to be cleaned regularly.

5. Noise Levels: Noise is an important consideration when choosing an AC system. Window units and portable air conditioners can be quite noisy, which might be distracting in bedrooms or living rooms. On the other hand, split systems and central air conditioning units are typically much quieter, as their noisy components are located outside the home. Mini-split systems are also known for their quiet operation since the indoor units are designed to be discreet and efficient.

6. Climate and Weather Conditions: The local climate plays a key role in the type of air conditioning system that will work best for you. If you live in an area with extreme heat and humidity, a more powerful system such as central air conditioning or a mini-split system may be necessary to maintain a comfortable indoor environment. In contrast, if you live in a region with milder temperatures, a smaller, more affordable window unit might be sufficient.

7. Smart Features and Technology: Many modern air conditioning systems come with smart features that allow you to control the temperature remotely via smartphone apps or smart home systems. These features can include programmable thermostats, scheduling, and the ability to adjust the temperature while you're away, saving energy. Some units also have sensors that detect when a room is empty and automatically adjust the cooling to save energy.

8. Environmental Impact and Refrigerants: Environmental concerns are increasingly important when choosing an AC system. Older air conditioning systems often use refrigerants that are harmful to the ozone layer and contribute to climate change. Look for systems that use eco-friendly refrigerants, such as R-410A, which are less damaging to the environment.

9. Brand Reputation and Warranty: When choosing an air conditioning system, it's essential to consider the brand's reputation for reliability and customer support. Look for trusted brands that offer strong warranties on parts and labor. A good warranty can provide peace of mind, ensuring that if anything goes wrong with the system, you are covered for repairs or replacements.

10. Aesthetics and Space Requirements: While functionality is the primary concern, the appearance and space requirements of the air conditioning system should also be considered. Some systems, like window units, are more noticeable, while others, like mini-splits or central AC, are more discreet and can blend in with the décor. Make sure to choose a system that fits your space, both in terms of physical installation and visual appeal. Choosing the right air conditioning system involves balancing factors such as the size of the space, energy efficiency, type of system, installation and maintenance costs, noise levels, and additional features. It is important to assess your specific needs, including the size of the area to be cooled, your budget, and long-term energy savings. Consulting with an HVAC professional can help you make the best decision, ensuring you select an air conditioning system that meets your comfort needs while being energy-efficient and cost-effective.

Part 5: HVAC Installation and Design

Chapter Ten: Designing an Efficient HVAC System for Your Space

Designing an efficient HVAC system for your space involves carefully planning how to heat, cool, and ventilate the environment while minimizing energy use and maintaining comfort. The goal is to create a system that provides the right temperature and air quality without wasting energy or increasing utility bills.

To design an efficient system, start by considering the size and layout of the space. The system needs to be properly sized to handle the cooling and heating demands of the area. An HVAC professional can help calculate the correct size by evaluating factors like square footage, insulation, number of windows, and how many people typically occupy the space.

Next, choose energy-efficient equipment, such as high-SEER air conditioners, energy-saving furnaces, and smart thermostats. These components help reduce energy consumption. Additionally, proper insulation and sealing of ducts and windows can prevent air leaks, keeping the conditioned air in and the outdoor air out.

Ventilation is another key factor in efficiency. Using a mix of natural and mechanical ventilation helps improve air quality without overworking the HVAC system. Finally, ensure regular maintenance and upgrades, such as changing filters and cleaning coils, to keep the system running smoothly and efficiently over time.

By carefully selecting equipment and considering the space's unique needs, you can design an HVAC system that is both effective and energy-efficient, providing comfort while reducing energy costs.

10.1 Sizing Your HVAC System (Load Calculations)

When installing or upgrading an HVAC system, one of the most important steps is determining the right size for the system. This is known as sizing the HVAC system, and it involves calculating the heating and cooling load requirements for your space. If the system is too small, it would not be able to heat or cool the space effectively. On the other hand, an oversized system can waste energy, lead to higher costs, and cause frequent cycling on and off, reducing the system's lifespan.

The process of sizing your HVAC system is done through load calculations. These calculations estimate how much heating or cooling your space needs based on several factors. Here is a detailed look at the process:

What is a Load Calculation

A load calculation is a process that determines the amount of heating or cooling your home or building requires to maintain a comfortable temperature. It considers various factors that influence the internal temperature, such as the size of the space, the insulation, the number of windows, the climate, and more. The result is used to choose an HVAC system with the appropriate capacity to handle those demands efficiently.

Factors Affecting Load Calculations

Several key factors affect the load calculation process:

a. Size of the Space: The total square footage of the area you want to heat or cool is a major factor. Larger spaces need more power from the HVAC system to regulate temperature.

b. Insulation: Well-insulated homes or buildings retain heat more effectively in the winter and stay cooler in the summer. Homes with poor insulation may need a larger HVAC system to compensate for heat loss or gain.

c. Number of Windows and Doors: Windows and doors can let in or out air, depending on the weather. The more windows and doors you have, the more heating or cooling the system will need to maintain the desired indoor temperature.

d. Building Orientation and Climate: The direction your building faces can affect how much sunlight enters through windows, which can influence how much heating or cooling is needed. In addition, the local climate (whether it's hot, cold, humid, or dry) will affect the system's capacity requirements.

e. Occupants and Activities: The number of people in the space can impact the load. People generate heat, so more occupants usually require more cooling. Similarly, activities like cooking, using electronics, or using heavy appliances can also affect temperature and increase load.

f. Air Leakage and Ventilation: Air leaks through cracks, gaps, and vents can result in heat loss in winter and heat gain in summer. Proper sealing of doors, windows, and ducts is necessary to reduce these losses and ensure the HVAC system works efficiently.

Tools Used for Load Calculations

Professionals use different tools and methods to perform accurate load calculations. One of the most widely used methods is the Manual J calculation, which is the industry standard for determining residential heating and cooling loads. Manual J takes into account all the factors mentioned earlier and provides an accurate calculation of the system's capacity requirements. For commercial buildings, larger load calculations may require more complex methods, such as Manual N or ASHRAE standards.

Types of Loads

Load calculations consider two types of loads:

a. Heating Load: This is the amount of heat required to maintain a comfortable indoor temperature during the colder months. It accounts for heat loss through walls, windows, ceilings, and doors, as well as the amount of heat generated inside the building by appliances and people.

b. Cooling Load: This refers to the amount of cooling needed to remove heat and moisture from the air in warmer months. It considers factors such as solar heat gain through windows, the outdoor temperature, the insulation quality, and internal heat sources like lighting and electronics.

Why Accurate Sizing is Important

Accurate sizing ensures your HVAC system works efficiently. If the system is too small, it will run constantly, struggling to maintain the desired temperature, leading to increased energy consumption, higher utility bills, and premature wear on the equipment. On the other hand, an oversized system will cycle on and off frequently, which not only wastes energy but also leads to discomfort due to uneven cooling or heating.

The Role of a Professional in Load Calculations

While some homeowners or business owners may attempt to estimate their HVAC needs, it is recommended to hire a professional HVAC technician to perform the load calculations. They have the knowledge and experience to consider all factors accurately and to use proper tools and software for precise calculations. This ensures the system is sized correctly for optimal performance and efficiency.

Sizing your HVAC system correctly through load calculations is crucial for both comfort and energy efficiency. By considering factors like space size, insulation, climate, and the number of occupants, a load calculation helps determine the ideal system size for your heating and cooling needs. This process ensures that the system will be effective, reliable, and energy-efficient, ultimately leading to lower utility bills and a longer lifespan for your HVAC equipment. Working with a professional is the best way to ensure the accuracy of your load calculations and choose the best system for your space.

10.2 Zoning for Comfort and Efficiency

Zoning is a method used in HVAC systems to divide a home or building into different areas, called "zones." Each zone can be controlled separately with its own thermostat, allowing for precise temperature regulation in different parts of the space. This approach offers several benefits, including enhanced comfort, energy efficiency, and the ability to tailor the HVAC system to the specific needs of each zone.

How Zoning Works

In a zoned HVAC system, the building is divided into multiple zones. These zones can be based on rooms, floors, or areas with different heating or cooling needs. For example, a house may have separate zones for the living room, bedrooms, kitchen, and basement.

Each zone is equipped with its own thermostat, allowing occupants to set the temperature that best suits their preferences for that specific area. The HVAC system uses dampers, which are mechanical devices placed in the ductwork, to control airflow to different zones. These dampers open or close based on the temperature settings for each zone, directing the heated or cooled air only to the areas that need it.

Benefits of Zoning

a. Enhanced Comfort: One of the biggest advantages of zoning is that it improves comfort by allowing you to set different temperatures for different areas of the home. For example, you may want the living room to be cooler during the day while keeping the bedrooms warmer at night. Zoning gives you the flexibility to create the ideal environment in each room without affecting the whole house.

b. Energy Efficiency: Zoning can significantly reduce energy usage by heating or cooling only the areas that need it, instead of wasting energy on unoccupied rooms. For example, if you're not using the guest room, you can adjust the thermostat to use less energy, saving on heating or cooling costs. This selective heating or cooling can lead to lower energy bills because you're not conditioning every room all the time.

c. Cost Savings: Since zoning allows for more efficient use of the HVAC system, it can result in lower utility bills over time. By avoiding over-conditioning unused areas, you can save on both heating and cooling costs. Though there may be a higher initial cost for the installation of a zoned system, the long-term savings in energy expenses can make it a cost-effective solution.

d. Increased System Longevity: Zoning helps reduce the strain on the HVAC system. When the system is running more efficiently, it does not have to work as hard to maintain a consistent temperature across the entire building. This can extend the lifespan of the HVAC equipment, as it reduces wear and tear caused by excessive use.

e. Personalized Temperature Control: In homes with multiple occupants, zoning allows everyone to adjust the temperature to their personal preference. For example, one family member may prefer a cooler bedroom, while another enjoys a warmer environment. Zoning gives everyone more control over their comfort without the need for constant adjustments to the thermostat.

Components of a Zoning System

i. Thermostats: Each zone has its own thermostat, allowing you to control the temperature for that specific area. Smart thermostats can be used for even more convenience, as they can be controlled remotely through an app on your phone or synced with other smart home systems.

ii. Dampers: Dampers are installed in the ductwork to control the flow of air to different zones. They open and close based on the settings from the thermostat, ensuring that only the needed amount of conditioned air reaches each zone.

iii. Zone Control Panel: The zone control panel is the central unit that manages the signals sent from each thermostat and adjusts the dampers accordingly. This control system is essential for ensuring that the HVAC system delivers the right amount of air to each zone at the correct temperature.

iv. Ductwork: Zoning requires a well-organized duct system to distribute air effectively to all the different zones. The ductwork needs to be designed to handle the airflow demands of each zone, and the dampers must be correctly placed to ensure the proper balance of airflow.

Types of Zoning Systems

a. Thermostatic Zoning: This is the most common type, where each zone has its own thermostat that controls the dampers and airflow.

b. Time-Based Zoning: In this system, different zones are conditioned based on time schedules. For example, the living room might be cooled during the day, and the bedrooms might be cooled at night.

c. Temperature-Based Zoning: Temperature-based systems adjust the airflow based on the readings from the zone's thermostat. The dampers adjust to open or close, depending on the temperature set on each thermostat.

Ideal Situations for Zoning

i. Large Homes: In bigger homes, certain areas may need more heating or cooling than others. For example, upper floors often heat up more than lower floors, and rooms with large windows may require more cooling. Zoning helps manage these differences efficiently.

ii. Multiple Floors: Homes with multiple floors often have uneven temperatures between floors, with upper floors getting hotter than lower floors. Zoning allows you to control the temperature in each floor separately, ensuring comfort throughout the house.

iii. Homes with Different Heating or Cooling Needs: Some rooms, like a kitchen or home office, might produce more heat than others due to appliances or equipment. Zoning allows these rooms to be cooled more effectively without overcooling other areas.

Zoning for comfort and efficiency in HVAC systems offers a variety of benefits, including enhanced comfort, energy savings, and improved system performance. By dividing a home or building into separate zones and allowing each zone to be controlled independently, zoning provides a tailored approach to heating and cooling that meets the specific needs of each area. With the right system in place, zoning can make your HVAC system more efficient, comfortable, and cost-effective.

10.3 Planning for Ductwork and Airflow

Planning ductwork and airflow is a critical part of designing an efficient HVAC system. Ductwork is the network of tubes that carries heated or cooled air throughout a home or building, and proper airflow ensures that air is distributed evenly and effectively. If the ductwork is poorly planned or airflow isn't optimized, it can lead to inefficiency, higher energy bills, and discomfort. Here is a detailed look at the process of planning for ductwork and airflow in an HVAC system.

Importance of Proper Ductwork Design

The ductwork in an HVAC system is responsible for delivering air to different rooms and zones of a building. How well this system is designed directly impacts how effectively the heating and cooling systems function. Poorly planned ducts can lead to air leaks, poor air distribution, and uneven temperatures.

Key factors in planning ductwork include:

i. Proper Sizing: Ducts must be the right size to carry the correct amount of air. If ducts are too small, the airflow is restricted, causing the system to work harder to push air through. If they're too large, it can result in energy waste and uneven air pressure.

ii. Airflow Efficiency: Efficient airflow ensures that conditioned air reaches the intended rooms without causing excessive pressure or energy loss. Proper airflow reduces the strain on the HVAC system and ensures it runs at its best.

How Ductwork Affects Airflow

Ductwork is designed to guide air from the HVAC unit to various areas of the building. The design of the ductwork affects how easily air can travel through the system. There are several components of ductwork that influence airflow:

a. Main Ducts: These are the primary pathways for air coming from the HVAC unit. They connect to the smaller ducts that distribute air to rooms or zones.

b. Branch Ducts: These are the secondary ducts that branch off from the main ducts to deliver air to in

dividual rooms. Proper placement and sizing of these branches are crucial for balanced airflow.

c. Duct Vents and Registers: These are the openings where air is delivered to the rooms. The size and location of vents affect how well the air circulates in the room.

d. Duct Material: The material used for ducts (such as sheet metal, fiberglass, or flexible ducts) affects airflow. Smooth surfaces (like metal ducts) allow air to flow more freely, while rough surfaces can create resistance and reduce airflow efficiency.

Factors to Consider When Planning Ductwork and Airflow

Several factors influence how you plan the ductwork and airflow

a. Size of the Building or Space: The larger the space, the more complex the ductwork system will be. Larger homes or commercial spaces require more ductwork to ensure that all rooms are properly conditioned. Proper sizing and layout are essential for efficient airflow.

b. Room Layout and Design: The layout of the rooms, including the number of floors, windows, and doors, affects airflow. For example, a room with many windows or large glass surfaces might require more airflow to maintain a comfortable temperature.

c. Airflow Balancing: Ensuring that air is evenly distributed across the building is important for comfort. If one area is getting too much air while another is getting too little, it can cause hot or cold spots. Balancing airflow involves adjusting the ducts and registers to ensure consistent temperatures throughout the building.

d. Duct Insulation: Insulating ducts helps maintain the temperature of the air as it travels through the system. Insulated ducts reduce energy loss and prevent air from heating up or cooling down before it reaches its destination.

e. Air Pressure: Proper planning of ductwork ensures that air pressure remains balanced. If there is too much pressure in certain ducts, it can lead to leaks or noisy operation. If the pressure is too low, air would not reach the rooms properly.

Ductwork Design Considerations

When planning ductwork, there are several key design aspects to consider:

i. Straight Ducts: Straight ducts allow air to flow more freely and are more efficient than ducts with many bends and turns. Keeping the ducts as straight as possible minimizes resistance to airflow.

ii. Proper Duct Sizing: Using the right size ducts for the amount of air that needs to be delivered is crucial. If ducts are too small, the airflow will be restricted, causing the system to work harder and use more energy. If ducts are too large, the air may move too quickly, leading to uneven temperature distribution.

iii. Minimizing Duct Length: The longer the duct, the more energy is needed to move air through it. Shorter ducts reduce the amount of energy lost during transport, making the system more efficient.

iv. Avoiding Kinks and Turns: Excessive kinks, bends, or sharp turns in the ducts can create resistance, reducing airflow efficiency. When planning the system, it's best to use gentle curves and avoid sharp angles.

v. Sealing Leaks: Ductwork must be properly sealed to prevent air leaks. Leaks in the ducts can lead to energy waste, as conditioned air escapes before it reaches the intended rooms. Leaky ducts also reduce system efficiency and can cause uneven heating or cooling.

Airflow Balancing and Control

Once the ducts are installed, airflow needs to be balanced. This means ensuring that each room or zone receives the right amount of air for comfort and efficiency. Airflow balancing can be done using:

a. Dampers: Dampers are adjustable valves that control the flow of air through the ducts. By adjusting the dampers, you can control how much air flows to each zone.

b. Registers and Vents: The size and placement of the vents and registers also affect airflow. Properly positioned vents ensure that air circulates properly, helping to maintain a consistent temperature throughout the space.

c. Zoning Systems: For larger spaces, a zoning system can be used to control airflow to different areas separately. Each zone can have its own thermostat and set temperature, which helps ensure that conditioned air is delivered only where it's needed.

Common Problems with Ductwork and Airflow

There are several common problems that can occur with ductwork and airflow:

a. Air Leaks: Leaky ducts cause air to escape, which leads to wasted energy and uneven temperature distribution. Sealing leaks is essential for efficiency.

b. Incorrect Sizing: Ducts that are too small or too large can cause problems with airflow. This can lead to discomfort, higher energy bills, and even damage to the HVAC system.

c. Clogged or Dirty Ducts: Dust and debris can accumulate in the ducts over time, restricting airflow and reducing system efficiency. Regular cleaning is important to keep ducts clear.

d. Improper Insulation: Ducts that are not insulated properly can lose a significant amount of energy, especially in unconditioned spaces like attics or basements. Insulating ducts helps maintain air temperature and improve system efficiency.

Proper planning for ductwork and airflow is crucial to ensuring an efficient, effective HVAC system. By designing ductwork that is properly sized, balanced, and sealed, you can achieve better airflow, reduced energy consumption, and consistent comfort throughout the building. Whether you are installing a new system or upgrading an existing one, careful attention to ductwork and airflow design will help your HVAC system perform at its best and provide long-term energy savings.

10.4 Considerations for Retrofitting vs. New Installations

When it comes to installing an HVAC system, there are two main options: retrofitting an existing system or installing a completely new one. Both approaches have their advantages and challenges, and the best choice depends on various factors, such as the condition of the existing system, the goals for energy efficiency, and the overall cost. Here is a breakdown of the key considerations for both retrofitting and new installations in HVAC.

1. Retrofitting an Existing HVAC System

Retrofitting refers to upgrading or modifying an existing HVAC system to improve its performance, efficiency, or capacity. It involves replacing or improving parts of the system while keeping most of the original setup in place.

Advantages of Retrofitting

a. Lower Initial Cost: Since retrofitting only involves upgrading parts of the system, the upfront cost is typically lower than a full replacement. You may be able to keep the existing ductwork, vents, and some equipment while upgrading key components such as the furnace, air conditioner, or thermostat.

b. Less Disruption: Retrofitting is usually less disruptive than a new installation because it doesn't require completely removing and replacing the entire system. This can be especially important in commercial buildings or homes where downtime or construction disruption is a concern.

c. Quicker Process: Since retrofitting uses many of the existing system's components, the installation time is typically shorter than a full replacement, meaning the system will be up and running sooner.

Disadvantages of Retrofitting

a. Limited Improvement: Retrofitting can improve efficiency and comfort, but it may not provide the same level of performance as a completely new system. Older systems have limitations in terms of technology and efficiency that may prevent them from being fully modernized.

b. Potential Compatibility Issues: Depending on the age and condition of the existing system, retrofitting may not always be possible or effective. For example, older ductwork or refrigerant types might not be compatible with newer energy-efficient equipment.

c. Ongoing Maintenance: While retrofitting can extend the life of an existing system, it may still require frequent repairs and maintenance. Older components may wear out more quickly, leading to additional costs over time.

2. New HVAC Installation

A new installation involves replacing the entire HVAC system, including the furnace, air conditioner, ductwork, and all other components. This approach is typically used when the existing system is outdated, inefficient, or beyond repair.

Advantages of New Installation

a. Energy Efficiency: New HVAC systems are designed with the latest technology and energy-saving features. Upgrading to a modern system can significantly reduce energy consumption and lower utility bills. Newer systems also use more environmentally-friendly refrigerants and other components.

b. Improved Comfort: A new system is often more effective at providing consistent and reliable comfort. Modern systems include features like variable-speed blowers, better humidity control, and advanced air filtration, all of which improve indoor air quality and comfort levels.

c. Longer Lifespan: New HVAC systems typically have a longer lifespan than retrofitted systems. With proper maintenance, they can last 15-20 years or more, while an older system that is been retrofitted may have a shorter remaining lifespan.

d. Better Performance: New systems are often more powerful and can handle larger spaces or changes in demand more effectively. They can provide better airflow, more precise temperature control, and a quieter operation compared to older systems.

Disadvantages of New Installation

i. Higher Upfront Costs: A new HVAC system requires a larger initial investment because it involves replacing the entire system. This includes the cost of purchasing new equipment, installing ductwork (if necessary), and labor costs.

ii. Longer Installation Time: Installing a new HVAC system typically takes more time than retrofitting. It may involve removing the old system, designing a new setup, and making modifications to the building, such as adding ductwork or upgrading the electrical system.

iii. Disruption During Installation: A full installation can be disruptive, especially in homes or commercial spaces that require major construction work. Dust, noise, and the removal of old equipment can create inconvenience during the installation process.

Key Considerations for Choosing Between Retrofitting and New Installation

a. Age and Condition of the Existing System: If the current HVAC system is relatively new and in good condition, retrofitting may be a cost-effective way to improve its performance. However, if the system is outdated or has frequent breakdowns, a new installation may be more cost-effective in the long run.

b. Energy Efficiency Goals: If energy efficiency is a priority, a new installation is often the better option. Modern systems are designed with advanced features that can provide significant energy savings over older systems, making a new installation the best choice for those seeking long-term efficiency.

c. Budget and Cost Considerations: Retrofitting tends to be more affordable initially, but it may not provide the same level of energy savings or performance as a new system. If you have a tight budget but still want to improve your system's efficiency, retrofitting may be a good compromise. However, if you can afford the higher upfront costs, a new installation could be the more economical choice over time.

d. Building or Home Size and Layout: In cases where the existing system isn't able to meet the needs of a growing building or home, a new installation may be necessary. New systems can be designed to handle larger spaces, and ductwork can be customized to fit the specific layout of the space.

e. Long-Term Value: While retrofitting can extend the life of your existing system, a new installation provides a longer lifespan and often greater reliability. If you plan to stay in the building for many years, investing in a new system may be worth the higher initial cost.

f. Comfort and Air Quality: New HVAC systems come with advanced features that can greatly improve indoor comfort and air quality, such as better filtration, humidity control, and zoning. If improving comfort is a priority, a new installation might be the best choice.

Whether to retrofit an existing HVAC system or install a new one depends on your specific needs, goals, and budget. Retrofitting can be a more affordable option for improving an older system, but it may not provide the same level of performance, efficiency, and longevity as a new system. On the other hand, a new installation offers modern features, higher energy efficiency, and better comfort, though it comes with higher initial costs and a longer installation time. By carefully considering factors such as system age, energy efficiency goals, budget, and comfort preferences, you can make the best choice for your home or business.

Chapter Eleven: Working with HVAC Professionals

When it comes to HVAC systems, whether you are installing a new one, upgrading an existing system, or maintaining an older one, working with HVAC professionals is essential. HVAC professionals are trained experts who understand the complex systems that provide heating, ventilation, and air conditioning in homes and businesses. They ensure that your HVAC system works efficiently, safely, and effectively. Here is a detailed guide on how to work with HVAC professionals and what to expect during the process.

1. Why You Need HVAC Professionals

HVAC systems involve intricate components such as thermostats, compressors, refrigerants, ductwork, and more. Handling these systems requires specific knowledge and training. While some basic maintenance tasks can be done by homeowners, tasks such as installation, repair, and system optimization should always be left to HVAC professionals. Here are a few reasons why working with experts is important:

a .Expertise and Experience: HVAC professionals have the knowledge and experience needed to handle all aspects of HVAC systems, from installation to repair and maintenance. They understand how each component works and can diagnose and fix issues that may not be immediately obvious.

b. Safety: HVAC systems involve electrical wiring, gas lines, and refrigerants, which can be dangerous if not handled properly. HVAC professionals are trained to work with these systems safely, minimizing the risk of accidents or damage.

c. Efficiency: A professional will help ensure that your HVAC system is installed or maintained correctly, leading to better energy efficiency and performance. A poorly installed system can result in increased energy costs and reduced comfort.

d. Compliance with Regulations: HVAC systems must meet local building codes and regulations. Professionals are familiar with these rules and ensure that installations and repairs are compliant, preventing potential fines or issues with your property.

2. When to Call an HVAC Professional

You may need to call an HVAC professional for a variety of reasons, including:

a. Installation of a New System: Installing a new HVAC system requires careful planning, proper sizing, and installation. An HVAC professional will evaluate your space, determine the correct system size, and ensure that it's installed properly.

b. Repairs: If your HVAC system is malfunctioning, it is important to call a professional. They can diagnose issues like strange noises, uneven temperatures, leaks, or system shutdowns, and provide the necessary repairs.

c. Maintenance: Regular maintenance helps keep your system running smoothly. HVAC professionals can perform tune-ups, clean filters, check refrigerants, and inspect components to prevent future problems.

d. Upgrades: If your system is outdated or inefficient, an HVAC professional can recommend upgrades such as a more energy-efficient furnace, air conditioner, or thermostat.

3. Finding a Reliable HVAC Professional

It is important to choose a trustworthy and reliable HVAC professional to ensure you get quality service. Here are some tips for finding the right one:

a. Check Qualifications: Look for HVAC contractors who are licensed, insured, and certified by recognized organizations, such as NATE (North American Technician Excellence) or ACCA (Air Conditioning Contractors of America). These certifications ensure that the technician is skilled and up to date on industry standards.

b. Ask for Recommendations: Ask friends, family, or neighbors if they have worked with an HVAC professional and can recommend someone. Positive word-of-mouth can help you find a trustworthy technician.

c. Read Reviews: Online reviews from customers can provide insights into the professional's quality of work, customer service, and reliability. Websites like Yelp, Google Reviews, or Angie's List can help you find a reputable HVAC professional in your area.

d. Get Multiple Quotes: For larger jobs like installation or repairs, it is a good idea to get multiple quotes from different HVAC professionals. Compare the costs, services, and warranties offered to ensure you are getting the best deal.

e. Verify Experience: Experience matters in HVAC work. Look for a professional who has been in business for several years and has experience working with systems similar to yours.

4. What to Expect During the Process

Once you have chosen an HVAC professional, it is important to understand what to expect during the process of installation, repair, or maintenance.

a. Consultation and Assessment: For new installations or major upgrades, the professional will first assess your space, your needs, and the existing system (if applicable). They will gather information about your home or business size, insulation, number of rooms, and any other factors that will affect the HVAC system's design and size. They may also ask about your budget and comfort preferences.

b. Estimation and Proposal: After the assessment, the HVAC professional will provide an estimate for the work required. This will include the cost of the system or components, labor, and any additional charges (permits or disposal fees). If it is a repair, they will inform you of the cost and get your approval before proceeding.

c. Installation or Repair: Once you approve the estimate, the HVAC professional will begin the installation or repair process. For new systems, this may involve removing the old system, installing new equipment, and connecting the ductwork, wiring, and refrigerant lines. For repairs, the technician will focus on diagnosing the problem and replacing faulty components.

d. Testing and Calibration: After installation or repair, the professional will test the system to ensure it is working properly. This may involve checking airflow, temperatures, refrigerant levels, and other critical components. They will also calibrate the system to ensure it is running efficiently.

e. Cleaning Up and Final Inspection: After the work is complete, the HVAC professional will clean up the work area and ensure that the system is in good working condition. They will review any maintenance tips with you and explain how to use and care for the system.

5. Maintenance and Ongoing Support

Once your HVAC system is installed or repaired, regular maintenance is key to ensuring it continues to work efficiently. HVAC professionals often offer maintenance contracts that provide scheduled inspections and tune-ups. Here's what to expect:

a. Scheduled Maintenance: Most HVAC professionals recommend annual or bi-annual maintenance for your system. Regular check-ups help identify and fix small problems before they become costly repairs.

b. Filter Replacement: During maintenance, the HVAC professional will replace or clean the air filters, which helps maintain air quality and system performance.

c. System Checkups: The technician will inspect key components such as the compressor, furnace, refrigerant levels, and ducts. They will also look for wear and tear that could lead to future breakdowns.

d. Troubleshooting: If something goes wrong with the system between maintenance visits, HVAC professionals are available to troubleshoot and repair any issues that arise.

6. Communication and Customer Service

Good communication is key to a successful relationship with an HVAC professional. Be clear about your needs, budget, and expectations. If you have any questions or concerns during the process, don't hesitate to ask the technician for clarification. A good HVAC professional will be happy to explain their work, offer advice on maintaining your system, and ensure that you're satisfied with the job.

Working with HVAC professionals ensures that your system is installed, repaired, or maintained correctly. By choosing a qualified, experienced, and reliable HVAC technician, you can rest assured that your heating, ventilation, and air conditioning needs will be met safely and efficiently. Whether you're looking for a new installation, repairs, or ongoing maintenance, these professionals help keep your HVAC system running smoothly for years to come.

Part 6: Maintenance and Troubleshooting

Chapter Twelve: Importance of Regular HVAC Maintenance

Regular HVAC maintenance is crucial for ensuring that your heating, ventilation, and air conditioning system runs efficiently, lasts longer, and operates safely. Just like any other mechanical system, HVAC units require periodic attention to keep them functioning at their best. Whether it is for your home or a commercial building, consistent maintenance helps avoid breakdowns, reduce energy costs, and maintain comfort. Here are the key reasons why regular HVAC maintenance is so important:

1. Improves Energy Efficiency: One of the main benefits of regular HVAC maintenance is improved energy efficiency. When your HVAC system is clean and well-maintained, it operates more efficiently, meaning it uses less energy to heat or cool your space. This can lead to significant savings on your utility bills. For example, dirty filters, clogged ducts, and poorly maintained components can force the system to work harder, increasing energy consumption. Regular maintenance ensures that everything is in good working order, optimizing energy use and lowering costs.

2. Prolongs the Life of Your HVAC System: Your HVAC system is a big investment, and you want to get as many years as possible out of it. Regular maintenance can extend the lifespan of your equipment. Components such as the compressor, motor, and coils can wear out over time, but routine inspections and servicing can catch issues before they become major problems. By addressing minor issues early, maintenance helps avoid expensive repairs and keeps your system running smoothly for a longer period.

3. Prevents Costly Breakdowns: Nothing is more inconvenient than an HVAC system that breaks down, especially during extreme weather conditions. Regular maintenance helps prevent sudden failures by identifying potential problems before they cause a complete breakdown. Technicians will inspect your system for wear and tear, check for leaks, and clean the parts that need it, such as filters and coils. This proactive approach can save you from emergency repair costs and keep your system running when you need it most.

4. Improves Indoor Air Quality: Your HVAC system does more than just control the temperature; it also helps regulate air quality. Regular maintenance includes cleaning and replacing filters, which improves the air quality inside your home or building. A dirty or clogged filter can trap dust, pollen, pet dander, and other allergens, circulating them throughout your space. Regular cleaning and replacing of filters help reduce allergens and pollutants, ensuring cleaner, healthier air.

5. Maintains Comfort Levels: A well-maintained HVAC system provides more consistent comfort throughout your home or building. Whether you're trying to stay warm in winter or cool in summer, regular maintenance ensures that your system can efficiently handle the temperature demands of your space. A system that's not well-maintained may struggle to reach the desired temperature, causing uneven heating or cooling. Regular inspections and tune-ups keep your system running at peak performance, providing consistent and reliable comfort.

6. Keeps Your System Safe: HVAC systems can involve electrical components, gas lines, and refrigerants, all of which can pose safety risks if not properly maintained. For example, a gas furnace that is not cleaned regularly can develop carbon monoxide leaks, which are hazardous to health. A technician will inspect all safety features during maintenance, including gas connections, electrical wiring, and venting systems, ensuring that everything is functioning properly. Regular maintenance helps identify potential safety issues and correct them before they lead to dangerous situations.

7. Optimizes System Performance: Routine maintenance keeps your HVAC system running at its best. During maintenance visits, professionals check the system's overall performance, including airflow, temperature regulation, and humidity control. They can calibrate the system to improve its performance and make adjustments to ensure it is working at the right capacity. This ensures that the system is operating at its optimal level, providing maximum comfort and efficiency.

8. Helps You Avoid Warranties Becoming Void: Many HVAC manufacturers require regular maintenance as part of the warranty agreement. If you don't keep up with regular maintenance, you might void your warranty, leaving you responsible for repair or replacement costs if something goes wrong. Keeping up with scheduled maintenance ensures that you comply with warranty requirements and protect your investment.

9. Saves Money in the Long Run Although regular HVAC maintenance comes with a cost, it is a small price to pay compared to the potential costs of repairs and energy bills. By catching issues early, you can avoid more expensive repairs in the future. A well-maintained system is also more energy-efficient, saving you money on utility bills. In the long run, regular maintenance is a cost-effective way to keep your HVAC system running efficiently and avoid larger, unexpected expenses.

10. Peace of Mind: Regular HVAC maintenance gives you peace of mind knowing that your system is in good shape. You won't have to worry about unexpected breakdowns or sudden spikes in energy costs. Plus, you'll be able to enjoy a comfortable environment without constantly thinking about your HVAC system. Regular HVAC maintenance is an essential part of owning and operating an HVAC system. It helps keep your system running efficiently, extends its lifespan, prevents costly breakdowns, improves indoor air quality, and ensures consistent comfort. By scheduling regular inspections and maintenance with a qualified professional, you can avoid major issues, reduce repair costs, and improve the overall performance of your HVAC system. It is an investment in both your home's comfort and your long-term saving

12.1 DIY Maintenance Tips

DIY maintenance for your HVAC system can help keep it running efficiently between professional service visits. One simple task is to regularly replace or clean the air filters, as clogged filters can reduce airflow and strain the system. You can also clean the outdoor unit by the following Tips

1. Cleaning and Replacing Air Filters

Cleaning and replacing air filters is one of the easiest and most important DIY maintenance tasks you can do for your HVAC system. The air filter is responsible for trapping dust, dirt, allergens, and other particles in the air, preventing them from circulating throughout your home or building. Over time, the filter can become clogged with debris, which can cause a number of issues for your HVAC system. Here's a detailed guide on how to clean or replace your air filters and why it is so important:

Why It is Important

The air filter plays a crucial role in maintaining both the efficiency of your HVAC system and the quality of the air inside your home. A dirty or clogged filter can reduce airflow, making it harder for your system to heat or cool your space effectively. This can lead to higher energy bills and increased wear and tear on the system. In addition, a clogged filter may allow dust, allergens, and other particles to circulate in the air, affecting indoor air quality. By regularly cleaning or replacing the air filter, you can keep your HVAC system running smoothly and improve the air you breathe.

How to Clean or Replace Your Air Filter

a. Turn off the HVAC System: Before you start, always turn off the power to your HVAC system to avoid any accidents or damage.

b. Locate the Air Filter: The air filter is usually located in the return air duct or near the blower motor. It is often housed in a rectangular or square slot and can be found near the furnace or air handler.

c. Remove the Filter: Once you have located the filter, carefully slide it out of its slot. Be gentle to avoid damaging the frame or the filter itself.

d. Check the Filter: Take a look at the filter to determine whether it needs cleaning or replacing. If the filter looks clean or only lightly dusty, it may only need a good cleaning. If it looks clogged or very dirty, it is best to replace it with a new one.

e. Cleaning the Filter (If Applicable): If you have a reusable filter, you can clean it with a vacuum or by washing it. If you're vacuuming, use a soft brush attachment to gently remove dust and debris. If you are washing it, rinse it under lukewarm water and allow it to dry completely before reinserting it into the system.

f. Replacing the Filter (If Necessary): If the filter is too dirty to clean or if it is disposable, replace it with a new filter of the same size and type. Most filters have a number printed on the side (like 16x20, 20x25) that indicates the size, so make sure to buy a filter that matches these dimensions. There are different types of filters, so choose one that fits your needs (HEPA filters for better air quality or standard fiberglass filters for basic filtration).

g. Reinstall the Filter: Once the filter is clean or replaced, carefully slide it back into its slot, ensuring it fits securely. Be sure to install the filter in the correct direction, as there are often an arrow on the filter that shows the airflow direction.

h. Turn the HVAC System Back On: After the filter is in place, turn your HVAC system back on and make sure it is working properly. You should notice an improvement in airflow and performance.

How Often Should You Clean or Replace the Filter

The frequency with which you need to clean or replace your air filter depends on several factors, such as the type of filter, the size of your home, the number of pets, and how often you use your HVAC system. As a general rule of thumb, you should check your filter every 1-3 months.

i. For standard fiberglass filters, they should be replaced every 30-60 days, especially during the heating or cooling seasons.

ii. For pleated filters (which tend to last longer), you can typically replace them every 3-6 months.

iii. For washable filters, clean them every 1-2 months, but always refer to the manufacturer's instructions for best practices.

If you have pets or allergies, you may need to change your filter more frequently, as pet dander and dust can clog the filter faster.

Benefits of Regular Filter Maintenance

a. Improved Air Quality: Clean filters help reduce the number of dust, pollen, pet dander, and other allergens in your indoor air, creating a healthier environment for you and your family.

b. Better Efficiency: A clean filter allows air to flow freely through the system, making your HVAC unit more efficient. This can lead to lower energy bills and less strain on your system.

c. Longer System Lifespan: By reducing the amount of dust and debris that enters your HVAC system, regular filter cleaning and replacement can help prevent wear and tear on the components, extending the lifespan of your system.

d. Consistent Comfort: With a clean filter, your HVAC system can more effectively maintain the desired temperature in your home, ensuring consistent heating and cooling performance.

Cleaning and replacing air filters is a simple yet essential task for keeping your HVAC system running smoothly. By performing this DIY maintenance regularly, you can improve the air quality in your home, boost your system's efficiency, and prevent costly repairs or replacements down the line. Remember to check the filter every few months, and replace or clean it as needed to keep your HVAC system in top condition.

2. Inspecting Ductwork and Vents

Inspecting ductwork and vents is an important DIY maintenance task that can improve the efficiency and air quality of your HVAC system. Ducts are the channels through which heated or cooled air flows throughout your home, and vents are the openings that deliver that air into individual rooms. Over time, ducts and vents can accumulate dust, dirt, and debris, or even develop leaks that reduce airflow and system performance. Regular inspection can help you identify problems early and address them before they lead to bigger issues.

Why It is Important

Inspecting ductwork and vents is crucial for several reasons. First, if there are leaks or blockages in the ducts, the air would not flow as efficiently, causing your HVAC system to work harder. This can lead to higher energy bills and reduce the lifespan of the system. Second, dirty ducts and vents can lower indoor air quality by circulating dust, mold, or allergens throughout your home. Lastly, if vents are blocked or obstructed, certain rooms may not receive the proper amount of heating or cooling, affecting comfort. Regular inspections help prevent these problems, ensuring your system runs efficiently and your indoor air remains clean.

How to Inspect Ductwork and Vents

1. Turn off the HVAC System: Before starting your inspection, always turn off your HVAC system to avoid any accidents or damage while working on it.

2. Check the Vents: Start by walking through your home and inspecting all the vents. Look for visible blockages such as dust buildup, furniture, or other objects that may be obstructing the airflow. Clean the vents with a vacuum cleaner or a damp cloth to remove dust, dirt, and debris. If you find any vents that are blocked by furniture, rearrange the space to allow for better airflow.

3. Inspect the Ductwork: Next, check the ducts. You may need to access the ductwork in areas such as the attic, basement, or crawl spaces. Look for visible signs of damage, such as holes, cracks, or disconnected sections. Leaky ducts allow air to escape, reducing efficiency and comfort. If you notice any leaks or holes, they can often be sealed using specialized duct tape or a duct sealant product. Make sure the seal is tight to prevent air from leaking out.

4. Look for Poor Insulation: Ductwork should be properly insulated to prevent energy loss. If you find areas where the insulation is damaged, missing, or worn, you should replace or repair it.

This helps maintain the temperature of the air traveling through the ducts, making the system more efficient and preventing energy waste.

5. Check for Condensation or Moisture: Inspect the ducts for any signs of condensation or moisture, as this can lead to mold or mildew growth. If you find moisture, it may be a sign of poor ventilation or an issue with your system. You may need to contact a professional to address this problem if it is extensive.

6. Inspect for Proper Ventilation: Ensure that all supply and return vents are open and not obstructed. Closed or blocked vents reduce airflow and can cause uneven temperatures in different rooms. Make sure vents are not painted shut or covered by curtains or furniture.

7. Seal Gaps and Leaks: If you find any small gaps or leaks in the ductwork that you cannot seal with tape, you may want to use a duct mastic or an aerosol sealant. For larger gaps or more significant damage, it might be best to call in a professional to repair the ductwork.

8. Consider a Professional Inspection: While inspecting ducts and vents is something you can do yourself, it is a good idea to schedule a professional inspection every few years. A technician can use specialized equipment to check for hidden leaks, blockages, or insulation issues that might not be visible during a basic DIY inspection.

Benefits of Inspecting Ductwork and Vents

a. Improved Energy Efficiency: Leaky ducts and blocked vents can cause your HVAC system to work harder, leading to higher energy bills. By sealing leaks and clearing blockages, you reduce strain on the system, helping it operate more efficiently and lowering energy costs.

b. Better Airflow and Comfort: When ducts and vents are clear and in good condition, air flows more easily throughout your home, leading to more consistent temperatures in every room. Proper airflow ensures that your HVAC system can heat or cool your space evenly, improving comfort.

c. Cleaner Air Quality: Over time, dust and debris can accumulate in the ductwork and vents. By inspecting and cleaning them regularly, you can reduce the amount of dust, allergens, and pollutants circulating in the air. This helps maintain better indoor air quality, which is especially important for people with allergies or respiratory issues.

d. Early Detection of Problems: Regular inspections allow you to catch small issues before they turn into bigger, more expensive problems. For example, a small leak in the ducts that is caught early can be easily sealed, but if ignored, it may lead to more serious damage that requires costly repairs.

e. Extended System Life: By ensuring that your ductwork is in good condition and working properly, you help your HVAC system run more smoothly and efficiently. This can extend the lifespan of your system by reducing strain on the components and preventing wear and tear.

Inspecting ductwork and vents is a simple yet essential DIY maintenance task that can improve the efficiency, comfort, and air quality of your HVAC system. By checking for blockages, leaks, and signs of damage, you can ensure that your system is working at its best. Regular inspections help prevent energy waste, improve airflow, and maintain cleaner air in your home. If you find any significant issues during your inspection, such as major leaks or extensive damage, it may be best to call in a professional for repairs. Overall, taking the time to inspect and maintain your ductwork and vents can save you money and help your HVAC system last longer.

3 Checking Thermostat Settings

Checking your thermostat settings is an important part of HVAC maintenance that can help ensure your heating and cooling system is running efficiently. The thermostat is the control center for your HVAC system, regulating the temperature by turning the system on and off. If the thermostat settings are incorrect or the thermostat isn't functioning properly, it can cause your HVAC system to work harder than necessary, leading to higher energy bills or uneven temperatures in your home. Here is a detailed guide on how to check and adjust your thermostat settings to keep your HVAC system working efficiently.

Why It is Important

A thermostat that's set incorrectly can cause your HVAC system to run more than it needs to, wasting energy and driving up utility costs. For example, if your thermostat is set too high in the summer or too low in the winter, your HVAC system will work overtime to try to reach the set temperature, leading to unnecessary energy use. By regularly checking your thermostat settings, you can ensure your system is operating as efficiently as possible and that your home remains comfortable. Additionally, an improperly functioning thermostat may cause inconsistent temperatures or prevent your system from reaching the desired temperature.

How to Check and Adjust Thermostat Settings

1. Turn off the HVAC System: Before you start adjusting the thermostat, make sure your HVAC system is turned off. This prevents the system from kicking in while you are making changes.

2. Check the Current Temperature: Look at the temperature reading on your thermostat. This will show you the current indoor temperature. Compare this to the temperature you want to maintain in your home.

3. Set the Desired Temperature: If the thermostat is set too high or too low, adjust it to the temperature you are comfortable with. In general, the U.S. Department of Energy recommends setting your thermostat to 78°F in the summer for cooling and 68°F in the winter for heating. If you are looking to save energy, try setting the temperature a few degrees higher in summer or lower in winter when you're not home or when you're sleeping.

4. Use Programmable or Smart Thermostat Settings: If you have a programmable thermostat, take advantage of its scheduling feature to automatically adjust the temperature based on your

routine. For example, set the temperature to be higher when you are away during the day and cooler when you are at home. For a smart thermostat, you can also control the temperature remotely from your phone or through voice commands. This helps maintain comfort while saving energy.

5. Check for Proper Mode: Ensure the thermostat is set to the correct mode for the season. In the summer, the thermostat should be set to "cool" mode to activate the air conditioning, while in the winter, it should be set to "heat" mode to turn on the furnace. Some thermostats also have an "auto" mode, which will automatically switch between heating and cooling depending on the temperature.

6. Calibrate the Thermostat: Sometimes, a thermostat may become miscalibrated, meaning it may not accurately reflect the temperature in your home. If the thermostat shows an incorrect reading, you can try to recalibrate it. Many digital thermostats come with a manual or an option to recalibrate, so refer to the manufacturer's instructions for guidance. If your thermostat is analog, you can use a separate thermometer to compare readings and adjust accordingly. If you cannot calibrate it yourself, it may be time to replace the thermostat.

7. Check for Battery Life: If you have a battery-powered thermostat, make sure the batteries are not running low. Low batteries can cause the thermostat to malfunction, leading to incorrect temperature readings or failure to control the HVAC system. Replace the batteries regularly to avoid issues.

8. Test the Thermostat: Once you have set the thermostat, turn the HVAC system back on and test the temperature. Set it to your desired temperature and wait for the system to respond. If it is working correctly, the heating or cooling system should kick in and begin adjusting the temperature toward the set point.

9. Look for Issues or Errors: If the thermostat is not responding or the temperature is not changing, there may be a problem with the thermostat. Check for any error codes or signs of damage, and consider calling a professional if the issue persists. It may need to be repaired or replaced.

Benefits of Checking Thermostat Settings

a. Improved Energy Efficiency: Setting the thermostat to the optimal temperature and adjusting it when needed can help your HVAC system run more efficiently, leading to lower energy bills.

b. Consistent Comfort: Proper thermostat settings ensure your home stays at a comfortable temperature throughout the day, preventing sudden temperature swings that can make your space uncomfortable.

c. Increased System Lifespan: By ensuring the thermostat is set correctly and operating efficiently, your HVAC system will not be overworked, which helps prevent excessive wear and tear and extends its lifespan.

d. Convenience and Automation: With a programmable or smart thermostat, you can set your system to adjust automatically, making it more convenient to maintain comfort and save energy without having to manually adjust the temperature.

e. Reduced System Wear and Tear: When the thermostat is functioning properly and set to an energy-efficient level, the system does not need to run as often or as long, reducing the risk of unnecessary breakdowns and repairs.

Checking and adjusting your thermostat settings is a simple yet effective DIY maintenance task that can improve the efficiency and performance of your HVAC system. By ensuring the thermostat is set to the correct temperature, using programmable features, and keeping it properly calibrated, you can maintain comfort in your home while saving on energy costs. Regularly inspecting your thermostat can also help prevent system malfunctions, ensuring your HVAC system works efficiently and lasts longer.

Chapter Thirteen: Common HVAC Problems and Solutions

Common HVAC problems can range from simple issues to more complex ones that may require professional help. Some of the most common problems include poor airflow, inconsistent temperatures, unusual noises, and system failures. Poor airflow could be caused by clogged air filters, blocked ducts, or malfunctioning fans. To solve this, you can clean or replace the filters and check for blockages in the ducts. If there is inconsistent heating or cooling, it might be due to thermostat issues, refrigerant leaks, or a malfunctioning compressor. Checking the thermostat settings and ensuring proper refrigerant levels can help resolve this. Unusual noises, such as rattling or buzzing, can indicate loose parts, a dirty fan, or motor issues, which may require cleaning or professional inspection. If your HVAC system is not turning on, the problem could be as simple as a tripped circuit breaker or as serious as a failed compressor. Regular maintenance, like cleaning filters, inspecting ducts, and servicing the system, can help prevent many common HVAC issues. If problems persist, it is always a good idea to consult an HVAC professional for further diagnosis and repair.

13.1 Uneven Heating or Cooling

Uneven heating or cooling is a common problem in many homes, where some rooms may feel too hot or too cold compared to others. This can be frustrating, as it leads to discomfort and may cause the HVAC system to work harder than necessary, leading to higher energy bills. There are several reasons why uneven temperatures may occur, and fortunately, many of these issues have simple solutions.

Causes of Uneven Heating or Cooling

a. Blocked or Closed Vents: One of the most common causes of uneven temperatures is blocked or closed vents. When vents are obstructed by furniture, rugs, or other objects, the airflow in that part of the house is restricted, causing certain rooms to get less heat or cool air. Similarly, if vents are accidentally closed, airflow is limited, resulting in uneven temperature distribution.

b. Dirty or Clogged Air Filters: Air filters trap dust, dirt, and other particles to prevent them from entering the HVAC system. Over time, these filters can become clogged with debris, which restricts airflow. When airflow is reduced, the HVAC system struggles to circulate air properly, leading to uneven heating or cooling.

c. Ductwork Issues: The ducts are the pathways that carry conditioned air throughout the house. If there are leaks, cracks, or blockages in the ductwork, air may escape or be blocked from reaching certain rooms. This can result in areas that are colder or warmer than the rest of the home. Poorly insulated ducts can also cause heat loss in the winter or heat gain in the summer, leading to uneven temperatures.

d. Improper Thermostat Settings: If the thermostat is located in an area of the home that is not representative of the overall temperature, it may cause the HVAC system to turn on or off too early or too late. For example, if the thermostat is placed near a heat source like the kitchen or in direct sunlight, it may sense the wrong temperature and fail to regulate the entire house properly.

e. Inadequate System Size: If the HVAC system is too small for the space it is trying to heat or cool, it would not be able to properly distribute air throughout the home. This can cause certain rooms to be too hot or too cold. Conversely, if the system is too large, it may cycle on and off too quickly, not allowing enough time for the air to circulate evenly.

f. Insulation Problems: Poor insulation in walls, windows, or attics can also cause uneven temperatures. Rooms with poor insulation may lose or gain heat more quickly than well-insulated rooms, resulting in temperature imbalances. Insufficient insulation can also cause drafts, which can make it harder for the HVAC system to maintain a consistent temperature.

Solutions to Uneven Heating or Cooling

1. Clear Blocked Vents: The first step is to check all the vents in your home and ensure they are open and unobstructed. Move furniture, rugs, or any other objects that may be blocking airflow. You can also adjust the position of the vents to help direct airflow where it is needed most.

2. Change or Clean the Air Filters: A simple fix for uneven heating or cooling is to clean or replace your HVAC system's air filters. Clogged filters can restrict airflow, causing the system to work harder. Replace filters regularly (typically every 1-3 months) to ensure smooth airflow and better efficiency.

3. Inspect and Seal Ductwork: Check the ducts for any visible leaks, cracks, or blockages. You can use duct tape or mastic sealant to seal small leaks, but for more extensive duct issues, it may be necessary to call a professional to repair or replace damaged sections. Sealing and insulating ducts can also improve energy efficiency and reduce temperature imbalances.

4. Reposition the Thermostat: If the thermostat is located in a hot or drafty area, it might not be sensing the correct temperature. Consider moving the thermostat to a more central location or away from heat sources like windows, direct sunlight, or appliances. Some modern thermostats also offer zoning capabilities, allowing you to control different areas of the house separately.

5. Balance the Airflow: If your home has multiple zones, consider installing zoning dampers in the ductwork. These dampers allow you to control airflow to specific areas of the home, ensuring more even heating or cooling in each room. A zoning system can be controlled by individual thermostats in different areas of the house, providing customized comfort.

6. Upgrade Your HVAC System: If your system is too small for your home or is aging, it may struggle to maintain consistent temperatures. In this case, upgrading to a larger or more efficient HVAC system can help. A professional can perform a load calculation to determine the right size for your space.

7. Improve Insulation: To prevent heat loss or gain and maintain a more even temperature, check the insulation in your home. Ensure that areas like attics, crawl spaces, and walls are properly

insulated. You may need to add insulation or weather stripping around windows and doors to improve efficiency and prevent drafts.

8. Install Ceiling Fans: Ceiling fans can help improve airflow in your home and help distribute conditioned air more evenly. In winter, set the fan to rotate clockwise to push warm air down, and in the summer, set it to rotate counterclockwise to cool the room.

Uneven heating or cooling is a common HVAC issue that can be caused by several factors, such as blocked vents, dirty filters, ductwork problems, and thermostat issues. Fortunately, there are simple solutions to improve airflow and achieve more consistent temperatures throughout your home. Regular maintenance, such as cleaning filters, inspecting ducts, and adjusting thermostat settings, can go a long way in improving comfort and energy efficiency. If the problem persists, it is a good idea to consult an HVAC professional to assess your system and make necessary repairs or upgrades.

13.2 Poor Airflow

Poor airflow is common HVAC problems that can make your home feel uncomfortable, and it often leads to the system working harder than necessary, which can increase energy costs. Airflow issues happen when the HVAC system is unable to circulate air efficiently throughout the home. This can cause certain rooms to feel stuffy, too warm, or too cold, and your HVAC system may seem like it is not cooling or heating the space as effectively as it should. There are several possible causes for poor airflow, but fortunately, many of these can be addressed through simple solutions.

Causes of Poor Airflow

a. Dirty or Clogged Air Filters: One of the most common causes of poor airflow is a dirty or clogged air filter. The air filter is responsible for trapping dust, dirt, and other debris before the air passes through the HVAC system. Over time, filters become clogged, which restricts the flow of air. When this happens, the system must work harder to push air through the filter, and you may notice reduced airflow in your home.

b. Blocked or Closed Vents: Vents are the openings in your walls or floors through which air flows into the rooms. If these vents are blocked by furniture, rugs, or other obstructions, the air can't flow freely. Similarly, if vents are closed or partially closed, it reduces the amount of air that can circulate in the room, leading to poor airflow.

c. Leaky or Damaged Ductwork: The ducts are responsible for carrying the conditioned air throughout the house. If there are leaks, cracks, or damage in the ducts, air can escape before it reaches its intended destination. This reduces the amount of air that flows into rooms, causing poor airflow and making it harder to heat or cool the space efficiently.

d. Dirty or Malfunctioning Blower Fan: The blower fan is an important component of the HVAC system that helps push air through the ducts and into your home. If the fan is dirty or not working properly, it would not be able to circulate air efficiently, leading to poor airflow. A malfunctioning blower can also cause the system to overheat or wear out faster.

e. Improperly Sized HVAC System: If your HVAC system is too small for your home, it may not be able to provide enough airflow to adequately heat or cool the entire space. On the other hand, an oversized HVAC system can cause uneven airflow, as it may cycle on and off too quickly without providing continuous, even air distribution.

f. Ductwork Design Issues: Sometimes, the problem lies in the design of the ductwork itself. If the ducts are too narrow or poorly positioned, they may not allow air to flow efficiently. Similarly, if the ducts are too long or contain many bends, it can create resistance to airflow, making it harder for air to travel through the system.

Solutions to Poor Airflow

1. Change or Clean the Air Filters: One of the easiest ways to improve airflow is to check and replace or clean your air filters. Air filters should be replaced every 1-3 months, depending on usage. If you have a reusable filter, make sure to clean it regularly to ensure proper airflow.

2. Clear Blocked Vents: Inspect all the vents in your home to ensure they are not blocked by furniture, curtains, or other objects. Move any obstacles away from the vents to allow for free airflow. Additionally, make sure all the vents are fully open. Some homeowners close vents in unused rooms to save energy, but this can create an imbalance in airflow and lead to poor circulation.

3. Inspect and Seal Ductwork: Check the ducts for any visible leaks, cracks, or loose connections. If you find any damage, you can seal the leaks with duct tape or mastic sealant. For larger repairs, you may need to call a professional to fix or replace sections of the ductwork. Sealing and insulating the ducts can improve airflow and energy efficiency, as well as prevent air loss.

4. Clean or Replace the Blower Fan: If the blower fan is dirty or malfunctioning, it can prevent the system from pushing air effectively. Make sure to clean the fan blades regularly to keep it running smoothly. If the fan is not working properly, you may need to call an HVAC technician to repair or replace it.

5. Consider an Upgrade or Adjustment to the System Size: If your HVAC system is too small or too large for your space, it can cause airflow problems. An HVAC professional can perform a load calculation to determine if your system is the right size for your home. If necessary, they may recommend upgrading or resizing the system to ensure better airflow and efficiency.

6. Improve Ductwork Design: If the ducts are poorly designed or installed, it can affect airflow. An HVAC technician can assess your system and make adjustments to improve the design. This might involve replacing narrow ducts with larger ones, rerouting ducts to more efficient locations, or adding dampers to balance airflow throughout the house.

7. Balance the Airflow: If you have a zoning system in place, it may need to be adjusted to balance the airflow across different areas of your home. Zoning systems allow you to control the temperature in different rooms or areas, but improper zoning can lead to airflow issues. A professional can adjust the system to ensure that each zone receives the proper amount of airflow.

8. Install an Air Circulation Fan: If certain rooms still experience poor airflow, consider installing additional fans to help circulate air. Ceiling fans, box fans, or oscillating fans can all help improve airflow in rooms where the HVAC system might not be distributing air as effectively.

Poor airflow can cause discomfort and inefficiency in your HVAC system. The good news is that there are several easy-to-fix causes, such as dirty filters, blocked vents, or leaky ducts. Regular maintenance, like cleaning filters, inspecting ducts, and ensuring the blower fan is working properly, can help prevent airflow issues. If the problem persists, it may be necessary to consult an HVAC professional who can assess and repair your system to restore proper airflow. Addressing airflow problems not only improves comfort but also boosts energy efficiency and extends the life of your HVAC system.

13.3 Noisy HVAC Systems

A noisy HVAC system can be a major source of discomfort in your home. While it is normal for HVAC systems to make some noise during operation, loud or unusual sounds can indicate underlying problems that need attention. Understanding the types of noises your system makes and their potential causes can help you address these issues and restore peace and comfort to your space.

Types of Noises and Their Causes

1. Banging Noises: A loud banging noise is often a sign of something loose or broken inside the HVAC system. This could be a loose blower fan, a broken motor mount, or an issue with the system's ducts. When parts like the fan or motor become loose, they may hit other components, creating a loud banging sound. In some cases, a dirty or clogged burner in the furnace can also cause a banging noise when the gas ignites.

2. Rattling Noises: Rattling sounds are often caused by loose components or parts inside the HVAC unit, such as the fan or panels. It could also be the result of a clogged air filter, which forces the system to work harder and causes parts to rattle. In some cases, debris or objects may have become trapped in the vents or ducts, causing rattling as air moves through them.

3. Squealing or Screeching Noises: High-pitched squealing or screeching sounds are often associated with problems with the fan or motor. Worn-out belts, a dirty blower fan, or a motor that is starting to fail can all produce squealing noises. This type of noise should be addressed quickly to prevent further damage to the components.

4. Hissing Noises: A hissing noise can be a sign of an issue with the refrigerant lines, a refrigerant leak, or a problem with the air ducts. If refrigerant levels are low due to a leak, the system will struggle to maintain proper cooling, and you may hear a hissing sound. Hissing can also occur if there's air escaping through damaged or poorly sealed ducts.

5. Gurgling Noises: Gurgling or bubbling sounds are commonly associated with refrigerant problems, particularly if the system is low on refrigerant. This issue may cause the system to fail in cooling your space properly, and it is essential to address it as soon as possible.

6. Thumping or Popping Noises: A thumping or popping noise can be a result of air moving through the ducts too forcefully, or it may be caused by a buildup of pressure in the ducts. This can occur when the air filter is clogged, restricting airflow, or if there is an issue with the blower fan that causes air to move unevenly through the ducts.

Solutions to Noisy HVAC Systems

a. Clean or Replace Air Filters: A clogged or dirty air filter is one of the most common causes of HVAC noise. When filters become clogged with dust and dirt, the system has to work harder to circulate air, which can lead to rattling, banging, or squealing sounds. Regularly replacing or cleaning the air filters can help reduce noise and keep your system running efficiently.

b. Tighten Loose Parts: Loose components inside the HVAC system, such as the blower fan or motor, can cause banging or rattling noises. Tightening loose screws or bolts may fix the problem. If you are not comfortable doing this yourself, it is best to call a professional to inspect and secure any loose parts.

c. Lubricate Moving Parts: Squealing or screeching noises are often caused by friction between moving parts, such as the fan or motor. Regularly lubricating these parts can help reduce friction and eliminate squealing noises. Be sure to follow the manufacturer's instructions when lubricating the system to avoid damaging any components.

d. Check and Seal Ducts: Leaking or poorly sealed ducts can cause hissing or gurgling sounds. Inspect the ducts for any visible holes or gaps, and use duct tape or mastic sealant to seal them. In some cases, ducts may need to be replaced if the damage is extensive. Sealing ducts also improves the overall efficiency of the HVAC system by preventing air loss.

e. Inspect the Fan and Blower Motor: A noisy fan or blower motor can cause a variety of sounds, including squealing, banging, or rattling. Check the fan blades for dirt or debris, and clean them if necessary. If the fan motor is worn out or malfunctioning, it may need to be replaced. A professional technician can help diagnose and repair these issues.

f. Check the Refrigerant Lines: If you hear a hissing or gurgling sound, it may indicate a refrigerant leak. Low refrigerant levels can cause the system to struggle to cool your home, leading to inefficient operation and noisy behavior. If you suspect a refrigerant leak, it is important to call an HVAC professional to inspect the system, fix the leak, and recharge the refrigerant.

g. Balance the Airflow: If the HVAC system is creating thumping or popping noises, it could be a result of pressure building up in the ducts due to poor airflow. Inspect the air filters, ductwork, and registers to ensure nothing is obstructing airflow. You may also need to have the system balanced or have the ducts cleaned to improve air distribution.

h. Schedule Regular Maintenance: Regular HVAC maintenance can help prevent many of the noise-related issues mentioned above. Having a professional inspect and tune up the system regularly will ensure that all components are working properly and efficiently. Routine maintenance can also catch small issues before they turn into larger, more expensive problems.

A noisy HVAC system can be annoying and disruptive, but in many cases, the cause can be traced back to a simple issue that can be fixed with regular maintenance or minor adjustments. Whether it is dirty filters, loose parts, or ductwork issues, addressing the source of the noise can help restore a quieter, more comfortable home. If the noise persists or you are unsure of the cause, it is always a good idea to call an HVAC professional to diagnose and repair the problem. Regular maintenance and timely repairs can help keep your HVAC system running smoothly and quietly for years to come.

Chapter Fourteen: When to Call a Professional

HVAC systems are complex machines that require proper care and maintenance to keep them running efficiently. While many minor HVAC issues can be handled by homeowners through regular maintenance or DIY fixes, there are certain situations where it is crucial to call a professional. Ignoring these problems or attempting to fix them yourself can lead to bigger, more expensive issues in the future. Here are some situations when it is best to call an HVAC professional.

1. Persistent System Issues: If your HVAC system is consistently not working properly, such as not heating or cooling effectively, or frequently cycling on and off, it may be time to call a professional. These persistent issues can be caused by a variety of underlying problems, like a faulty thermostat, refrigerant leaks, or a malfunctioning component. A professional technician can diagnose and repair these problems to restore your system's efficiency and performance.

2. Low Refrigerant Levels: If you notice that your air conditioning is not cooling as effectively as it used to, or if you hear a hissing sound coming from the system, you may have a refrigerant leak. Refrigerant is a crucial part of the cooling process, and low levels can lead to poor cooling performance, higher energy bills, and potential damage to the compressor. Refrigerant issues should only be handled by a certified HVAC professional, as they require specific training and tools to repair and recharge the system safely.

3. Noisy HVAC System: A noisy HVAC system, such as squealing, banging, or rattling, could indicate a more serious problem. These noises may be a sign of loose or broken parts, worn-out belts, or problems with the blower motor. If the noise persists after basic checks and cleaning, it is a good idea to call a professional. Continuing to run a noisy system can cause further damage, and an HVAC technician can quickly identify and fix the issue.

4. Airflow Problems: If you notice poor airflow throughout your home, or if some rooms feel much colder or hotter than others, there may be an issue with the ductwork, blower motor, or air handler. While homeowners can inspect and clean air filters and vents, airflow problems that go beyond simple blockages often require the expertise of a professional. A technician can inspect the ducts, fan, and other components to identify the cause of the airflow issue and recommend the appropriate solution.

5. Frozen Coils: If your air conditioner or heat pump has frozen coils, it is usually a sign of a deeper problem, such as low refrigerant levels, poor airflow, or a malfunctioning thermostat. A frozen coil can stop the system from cooling properly and can cause long-term damage if not addressed. If you notice ice forming on your HVAC system's coils, it is time to call a professional for an inspection and repair.

6. Water Leaks: Water leakage around the HVAC unit can indicate problems such as a clogged condensate drain or a refrigerant leak. While a small amount of water leakage may not seem alarming, it can lead to bigger problems like mold growth, water damage, and system

malfunction. If you see water pooling around the unit or dripping from the system, it is best to call a professional to prevent further damage.

7. Electrical Problems: If your HVAC system is experiencing electrical issues, such as tripping circuit breakers, blowing fuses, or problems with the thermostat, it is important to call a licensed HVAC technician. Electrical issues can be dangerous and should never be handled by anyone other than a trained professional. An expert can safely diagnose and fix electrical problems, preventing potential hazards and further damage to the system.

8. Old or Outdated System: As your HVAC system ages, it may start experiencing more frequent issues, such as inefficiency, rising repair costs, or difficulty keeping your home comfortable. If your system is over 10 years old and you find that repairs are becoming more common or expensive, it might be time to consider replacing it. An HVAC professional can help assess whether repairs or a full replacement would be more cost-effective in the long run.

9. Emergency Repairs: In some cases, you may experience an HVAC emergency, such as a complete system breakdown in the middle of a heat wave or during winter. If your heating or cooling system stops working entirely, it is important to call a professional immediately to avoid discomfort or safety risks. HVAC professionals are equipped to handle emergencies and can quickly get your system up and running again.

10. Lack of Comfort: If your home feels uncomfortable despite your HVAC system running, it could be due to issues like poor humidity control, uneven temperatures, or the system not reaching the desired temperature. A professional can assess your system and make adjustments to ensure your home stays comfortable year-round. This might involve recalibrating the thermostat, repairing a malfunctioning sensor, or adjusting airflow to different rooms.

11. Foul Odors: Strange odors, such as musty smells, burning odors, or something similar to rotten eggs, can indicate problems within the HVAC system. A musty smell could mean mold growth in the ducts or the air handler, while a burning smell might suggest an electrical issue or a problem with the motor. If you detect any unusual odors, it is best to contact an HVAC technician for an inspection and repair.

While there are several HVAC issues that homeowners can address themselves, there are times when calling a professional is the best course of action. Whether it is for a serious refrigerant leak, persistent system malfunctions, or issues with airflow, an experienced HVAC technician can provide the expertise needed to diagnose and fix the problem. Timely intervention from a professional can not only restore comfort to your home but also help prevent further damage, extend the lifespan of your system, and improve energy efficiency. If you ever feel unsure or uncomfortable handling HVAC problems on your own, do not hesitate to reach out to a trusted professional for help.

Part 7: Energy Efficiency and Sustainability

Chapter Fifteen: Understanding HVAC Energy Ratings (SEER, HSPF, AFUE)

When shopping for or maintaining an HVAC system, it is important to understand energy ratings. These ratings help consumers evaluate the efficiency of different HVAC units, which can save money on energy bills and reduce environmental impact. The three key energy ratings to look for are SEER, HSPF, and AFUE. Each rating applies to different components of an HVAC system, helping you make an informed decision when it comes to heating and cooling your home.

1. SEER (Seasonal Energy Efficiency Ratio)

SEER is a rating used to measure the energy efficiency of air conditioners and heat pumps during the cooling season. The higher the SEER rating, the more efficient the system is at cooling your home. It is calculated by dividing the cooling output (measured in BTUs) by the amount of energy the unit consumes (measured in watt-hours) over the course of an entire cooling season.

a. How it works: For example, if an air conditioner has a SEER of 16, it means that for every unit of energy it consumes, it provides 16 units of cooling.

b. Why it is important: A higher SEER rating typically means that the air conditioner will use less energy to cool your home, which results in lower electricity bills. More efficient systems are also better for the environment since they use less energy.

2. HSPF (Heating Seasonal Performance Factor)

HSPF is the energy efficiency rating used for heat pumps in heating mode. It measures the efficiency of a heat pump to provide heating during the winter months. The higher the HSPF, the more efficient the heat pump is at converting energy into heat. Similar to SEER for cooling, HSPF gives consumers an idea of how much heating they can get from the energy the system consumes.

a. How it works: To calculate HSPF, you divide the total heating output (measured in BTUs) by the total energy consumed (measured in watt-hours) during the heating season. A higher HSPF rating means more efficient heating.

b. Why it is important: Heat pumps with a higher HSPF will cost less to operate and can provide more heating power for the same amount of energy. This makes them an ideal choice for areas with mild winters where efficiency is important.

3. AFUE (Annual Fuel Utilization Efficiency)

AFUE is a rating that measures the efficiency of heating systems, specifically furnaces and boilers. It indicates the percentage of the fuel (typically gas, oil, or propane) that is converted into heat for your home. For example, if a furnace has an AFUE rating of 90%, it means that 90% of the fuel is converted into useful heat, and the remaining 10% is lost as waste.

a. How it works: AFUE is calculated based on the total energy input and the heat output over the course of a year. A higher AFUE means better energy efficiency.

b. Why it is important: A higher AFUE rating means that your heating system is more efficient at turning fuel into heat. This results in lower energy bills and reduces the amount of fuel you need to heat your home. Systems with high AFUE ratings are also better for the environment because they waste less energy.

Comparing SEER, HSPF, and AFUE

While SEER, HSPF, and AFUE are all used to measure the efficiency of HVAC systems, each rating applies to different types of units:

a. SEER is used for air conditioners and heat pumps during the cooling season.

b. HSPF is specifically for heat pumps when they are used for heating.

c. AFUE applies to heating systems like furnaces and boilers.

Each rating helps you compare the energy efficiency of different systems to determine which one will be the most cost-effective and environmentally friendly option for your home.

Why Understanding These Ratings Matters

Understanding SEER, HSPF, and AFUE ratings is essential for making smart decisions about your HVAC system. A higher rating means the system uses less energy to do the same job, resulting in lower energy bills. Over time, choosing an energy-efficient HVAC system can pay off in savings, and it also helps reduce your carbon footprint. If you are upgrading or installing a new HVAC system, always check these ratings and consider how they align with your energy efficiency goals.

In addition to the ratings, it is important to think about the climate and size of your home. In warmer climates, SEER may be the most important, while in colder climates, HSPF and AFUE may be more relevant. Always consult with an HVAC professional to determine the best system and energy ratings for your specific needs.

15.1 Tips for Improving HVAC Energy Efficiency

Improving the energy efficiency of your HVAC system can help you save money on energy bills and reduce your environmental impact. Regular maintenance is one of the easiest ways to improve efficiency, such as changing air filters and scheduling annual professional inspections. Upgrading to a high-efficiency HVAC system can also make a big difference, especially if your current system is older. Sealing leaks around windows and doors, adding insulation, and ensuring proper ductwork can prevent energy loss and reduce strain on your system. Using a programmable thermostat helps you control energy use by adjusting the temperature when you're not home or asleep. Lastly, consider using ceiling fans to help circulate air, which reduces the need for constant heating or cooling from your HVAC system. These simple changes can make your home more comfortable while lowering your energy costs.

1. Smart Thermostats

Smart thermostats are a great way to improve the energy efficiency of your HVAC system. These modern devices are designed to help you control the temperature of your home more effectively, saving both energy and money. Unlike traditional thermostats, which require manual adjustments, smart thermostats can be programmed to adjust temperatures automatically based on your schedule and preferences.

One of the main benefits of a smart thermostat is its ability to learn from your daily routine. For example, it can learn when you're typically home or away, and adjust the temperature accordingly. This means your HVAC system would not be running at full power when no one is around, which can lead to significant energy savings. It can also adjust the temperature based on the time of day, so it can be cooler at night when you are sleeping or warmer in the morning before you wake up.

Many smart thermostats can be controlled remotely using a smart phone app, which allows you to adjust the temperature even when you're not at home. This can be especially useful if your plans change, and you need to adjust the temperature before you return home. Some smart thermostats even work with voice assistants allowing you to control the temperature with simple voice commands.

Another advantage of smart thermostats is their ability to provide detailed energy usage reports. You can see how much energy you're using, when your system is running, and how much you are spending. This information can help you make better decisions about your heating and cooling habits, leading to more efficient energy use.

In addition to these features, many smart thermostats are compatible with a variety of HVAC systems, including central air conditioning, heat pumps, and furnaces. Some models also offer advanced features like geofencing, which adjusts the temperature when it detects that you are leaving or returning home based on the location of your phone.

Overall, installing a smart thermostat can make a significant difference in your home's energy efficiency. It not only helps reduce energy consumption but also provides convenience and control over your home's climate. By setting it up to match your schedule and habits, you can enjoy a comfortable living environment while keeping energy costs low.

2. Insulation and Sealing

Insulation and sealing are key factors in improving the energy efficiency of your HVAC system. They work together to keep the air inside your home at the right temperature, reducing the need for your HVAC system to work harder. Proper insulation and sealing prevent heated or cooled air from escaping, which can save you a lot of energy and money.

Insulation works by slowing the flow of heat. In the winter, it helps keep the warm air inside, and in the summer, it keeps the cool air in. Insulation is especially important in areas like the attic, walls, and floors. When these areas are well-insulated, your HVAC system doesn't have to work as hard to maintain a comfortable temperature. For example, if your attic is poorly insulated, a lot of heat can escape in the winter, making your furnace work harder. In the summer, poor insulation allows heat from the outside to enter your home, causing your air conditioner to use more energy to cool the space.

Sealing is also crucial for energy efficiency. Over time, gaps and cracks can form around windows, doors, and even the ducts that carry air throughout your home. These gaps let conditioned air escape and allow outdoor air to enter, which forces your HVAC system to work overtime to maintain your desired temperature. Sealing these leaks is a simple and cost-effective way to improve energy efficiency. Common areas to check for leaks include around windows, doors, and duct joints.

To properly insulate your home, start by adding insulation to the attic, as it is one of the most common places for heat loss. You can also insulate walls, floors, and basements, especially if your home has an unfinished basement or crawl space. There are different types of insulation, including fiberglass insulation, spray foam insulation, and blown-in cellulose insulation. Each type works well in different areas, so it's important to choose the right one for your needs.

Sealing should be done around windows and doors, where drafts are most common. Weather stripping or caulking can be used to seal gaps and prevent air leaks. It's also important to check your ductwork for any cracks or holes. You can use mastic sealant or specialized tape to seal these gaps. Sealing ducts properly ensures that the air reaches the right places without any loss along the way.

By improving insulation and sealing, you can reduce the workload on your HVAC system, which in turn improves its efficiency. This will not only help keep your home comfortable year-round but also lower your energy bills. With just a few simple changes, you can make your home more energy-efficient and enjoy the benefits of a more effective HVAC system.

15.2 Introduction to Green HVAC Technologies

Green HVAC technologies are designed to improve energy efficiency while minimizing environmental impact. These systems focus on using sustainable energy sources, reducing energy consumption, and cutting down on harmful emissions. Green HVAC solutions can include high-efficiency equipment, such as energy-saving air conditioners and heaters, as well as renewable energy sources like solar and geothermal energy. They also prioritize smart systems like programmable thermostats, which help optimize energy use. In addition, green HVAC systems aim to reduce waste and improve indoor air quality by using eco-friendly materials and better ventilation. Overall, these technologies not only help reduce energy costs but also contribute to a cleaner, more sustainable environment.

1. Renewable Energy Integration (Solar-Powered HVAC)

Solar-powered HVAC systems are an innovative and sustainable way to reduce energy consumption and environmental impact. By integrating solar energy with your heating, ventilation, and air conditioning system, you can harness the power of the sun to run your HVAC system more efficiently, potentially eliminating or significantly reducing your reliance on traditional energy sources like electricity or gas.

In a solar-powered HVAC system, solar panels are installed on the roof or another area with direct exposure to sunlight. These panels capture sunlight and convert it into electricity, which is then used to power your HVAC system. Depending on the system setup, solar power can either fully or partially power your HVAC unit, helping to lower energy bills and reduce your carbon footprint.

Solar-powered HVAC systems are particularly effective in sunny climates, where they can generate a significant amount of energy. For example, solar panels can provide enough electricity to run air conditioning units during the hot summer months, when cooling needs are highest. Additionally, solar water heating systems can be integrated into HVAC systems to provide hot water, further improving energy efficiency and reducing reliance on conventional energy sources.

One of the main benefits of solar-powered HVAC systems is that they rely on renewable energy, meaning they don't deplete natural resources or produce harmful greenhouse gases. This makes them an environmentally friendly choice for homeowners and businesses looking to reduce their carbon footprint and contribute to sustainability efforts.

Another advantage is that solar energy is free once the system is installed, which can lead to long-term savings on energy bills. While the initial cost of installing a solar-powered HVAC system may be higher than traditional systems, the energy savings over time can offset this cost. Additionally, many regions offer incentives and rebates for renewable energy installations, making it more affordable for homeowners to make the switch.

However, it is important to consider that solar-powered HVAC systems are dependent on sunlight, which means they may not always provide a consistent power source, especially during cloudy days or at night. To address this, many systems are paired with battery storage systems that store excess energy generated during the day for use at night or on cloudy days.

In conclusion, integrating renewable energy like solar power into HVAC systems is an excellent way to reduce energy costs, improve efficiency, and promote environmental sustainability. Solar-powered HVAC systems not only offer long-term savings but also contribute to reducing reliance on fossil fuels, making them a smart and eco-friendly choice for homeowners looking to embrace green technology.

2. High-Efficiency Systems

High-efficiency HVAC systems are designed to provide optimal comfort while consuming less energy, helping to reduce environmental impact and save money on energy bills. These systems use advanced technology and engineering to perform the same tasks heating, cooling, and ventilation as traditional systems, but with much less energy.

One of the key features of high-efficiency systems is their ability to use less electricity or fuel while providing the same level of comfort. This is achieved through components like high-efficiency compressors, fans, and heat exchangers, which work together to improve performance and minimize energy waste. These systems are built to run longer without using excessive amounts of energy, reducing the need for constant operation and lowering overall energy consumption.

A common example of a high-efficiency system is a high-efficiency furnace or air conditioner. These systems are rated with a higher Seasonal Energy Efficiency Ratio (SEER) for air conditioners or Annual Fuel Utilization Efficiency (AFUE) for furnaces. The higher these ratings, the more energy-efficient the system is. For example, a high-efficiency furnace may convert up to 98% of the fuel it uses into heat, while a standard model may only achieve 80% efficiency. This means less energy is wasted, and your home stays comfortable while using less energy.

In addition to energy savings, high-efficiency HVAC systems often offer better performance and enhanced indoor air quality. For example, modern high-efficiency air conditioners use advanced filtration systems that help remove dust, allergens, and other pollutants from the air, improving air quality and making your home healthier.

Another benefit of high-efficiency systems is that they often come with advanced features, such as variable-speed motors and modulating heat systems. These features allow the system to adjust its output to match the actual needs of the home, rather than running at full capacity all the time.

This means the system uses energy only when necessary, helping to maintain comfort without wasting energy.

Though high-efficiency systems typically come with a higher upfront cost compared to traditional HVAC systems, they pay for themselves over time through energy savings. Many homeowners find that the savings on utility bills more than offset the initial cost of installation. Additionally, many regions offer rebates and tax incentives for installing energy-efficient systems, which can further reduce the financial burden.

In summary, high-efficiency HVAC systems offer a smart and sustainable way to keep your home comfortable while reducing energy use and environmental impact. By investing in these systems, you not only save money on energy bills but also contribute to a more sustainable and eco-friendly future.

15.3 Rebates and Incentives for Energy-Efficient HVAC Upgrades

Upgrading to an energy-efficient HVAC system can be a smart investment, as it helps reduce energy bills and lowers your carbon footprint. However, the initial cost of purchasing and installing an energy-efficient system can be a bit higher compared to traditional systems. Fortunately, many governments, utilities, and manufacturers offer rebates and incentives to encourage homeowners and businesses to make the switch to more energy-efficient options.

Rebates are financial incentives provided by utility companies, local governments, or energy efficiency programs that help reduce the upfront cost of purchasing and installing energy-efficient HVAC systems. These rebates are typically offered for systems that meet specific energy-efficiency standards, such as those certified by ENERGY STAR, a program run by the U.S. Environmental Protection Agency (EPA). ENERGY STAR-certified systems are known for their high energy efficiency and are a popular choice for homeowners looking to upgrade their HVAC systems.

In addition to rebates, there are often tax incentives available for energy-efficient home improvements. For example, some local, state, or federal programs provide tax credits that reduce the amount of income tax you owe. These incentives are typically designed to encourage homeowners to invest in eco-friendly technologies, like high-efficiency HVAC systems, which help lower overall energy consumption and reduce greenhouse gas emissions.

The specific rebates and incentives available can vary depending on your location and the type of HVAC system you're installing. Utility companies, for example, often offer rebates for energy-efficient systems like high-efficiency furnaces, air conditioners, or heat pumps. These rebates are usually offered on a first-come, first-served basis, so it is a good idea to check with your local utility provider to find out about current offers.

In some cases, you may also be eligible for financing programs that make the upfront cost of upgrading to an energy-efficient system more manageable. These programs often offer low-interest loans or even deferred payment plans, allowing you to pay off the cost of the system over time. Some financing programs are specifically targeted at homeowners who are upgrading their systems to improve energy efficiency or reduce energy consumption.

To take full advantage of rebates and incentives, it is important to keep documentation of your purchase, installation, and any applicable energy efficiency certifications. Many rebate programs and incentives require proof that the system meets certain efficiency standards, so saving your receipts and installation records will help ensure you receive the full benefit.

In addition to these financial incentives, many homeowners also experience long-term savings on energy bills as a result of their energy-efficient HVAC systems. These systems are designed to use less energy while providing the same level of comfort, so the money saved on utilities can help offset the cost of the upgrade.

In conclusion, upgrading to an energy-efficient HVAC system is a smart choice for both your wallet and the environment. Thanks to rebates, tax incentives, and financing programs, it is easier than ever to make the switch to a more energy-efficient system. Be sure to explore all available options and take advantage of the savings to enjoy a more comfortable, eco-friendly home while reducing your energy costs.

Part 8: Safety and Regulations

Chapter Sixteen: HVAC Safety Tips for Homeowners

HVAC systems are essential for maintaining comfort in your home, but they also require careful attention to ensure safety and optimal performance. By following some simple safety tips, you can prevent potential hazards, protect your system, and keep your home comfortable. Here are some important HVAC safety tips every homeowner should keep in mind:

1. Schedule Regular Maintenance One of the best ways to ensure your HVAC system runs safely and efficiently is to have it professionally serviced at least once a year. Regular maintenance helps identify potential issues before they become major problems, such as gas leaks, electrical faults, or worn-out parts. An HVAC technician will inspect the system, clean the components, and make necessary adjustments to keep everything running smoothly.

2. Change Air Filters Regularly Air filters are crucial for maintaining good air quality and efficient system operation. Clogged or dirty filters can restrict airflow, causing the system to work harder and potentially overheat. This can lead to equipment failure or even fires in extreme cases. To avoid this, check and replace the air filters every 1-3 months, especially during peak usage seasons (summer and winter).

3. Check the Thermostat Settings Sometimes, HVAC issues are linked to improper thermostat settings. Ensure your thermostat is set to the right temperature and is functioning properly. If you notice temperature fluctuations or your system not responding, it may be time to recalibrate the thermostat or replace the batteries. This will ensure your HVAC system operates efficiently and does not overwork itself.

4. Inspect Ductwork and Vents Over time, dust and debris can accumulate in the ducts and vents, which can affect airflow and air quality. It is important to regularly inspect the ducts for leaks, blockages, or damage. Leaky ducts can lead to energy loss and poor performance. Also, make sure vents are unobstructed by furniture, curtains, or other items, as this can cause poor air distribution and strain on the system.

5. Check for Gas Leaks (For Gas Furnaces) If your HVAC system uses natural gas, it is essential to check for gas leaks regularly. A gas leak can be dangerous and lead to serious health risks, fires, or even explosions. If you smell gas or hear a hissing sound near your furnace, turn off the gas supply immediately and contact a professional HVAC technician for an inspection. Never attempt to repair a gas leak yourself.

6. Ensure Proper Ventilation Proper ventilation is key to safety, especially in systems that involve combustion, such as gas furnaces or water heaters. Make sure that air vents and flues are clear of obstructions and allow for proper exhaust. Blocked vents can cause dangerous carbon monoxide buildup, which is harmful and potentially fatal. Install carbon monoxide detectors in areas near your furnace or water heater to alert you of any dangerous gas buildup.

7. Clean and Maintain Outdoor Units Outdoor units, like air conditioning condensers, should also be maintained to ensure safe operation. Remove leaves, dirt, and debris that can accumulate

around the unit, which can block airflow and cause the system to overheat. Make sure the unit is placed on a level surface and that it has enough clearance for proper air circulation.

8. Avoid DIY Repairs While it might seem tempting to fix a minor issue with your HVAC system yourself, it is always best to call a professional. HVAC systems are complex, and attempting repairs without the right knowledge or tools can lead to further damage, costly repairs, or even accidents. Always hire a licensed HVAC technician for repairs and installations to ensure the job is done safely and correctly.

9. Be Mindful of Electrical Safety HVAC systems involve electrical components, and it is important to ensure everything is in good working order. Never attempt to handle electrical components without turning off the power first. If you notice anything unusual, like sparks, strange smells, or tripped circuit breakers, contact an electrician or HVAC professional immediately to avoid electrical hazards.

10. Know How to Shut Off the System In case of an emergency, it is important to know how to quickly turn off your HVAC system. Familiarize yourself with the location of the shutoff valve for the gas and the power switch for the system. This knowledge can be crucial if there is a problem like a gas leak, electrical issue, or fire risk.

By following these HVAC safety tips, you can ensure your system runs smoothly and safely, protecting both your home and your family. Regular maintenance, inspections, and timely repairs can extend the life of your HVAC system, improve energy efficiency, and prevent costly or dangerous problems. Always remember that safety should come first when it comes to your HVAC system.

16.1 Understanding Building Codes and Standards

Understanding building codes and standards in HVAC is essential for ensuring that your heating, ventilation, and air conditioning system is installed, maintained, and operates safely and efficiently. Building codes are a set of local laws and regulations that outline the minimum requirements for HVAC systems to meet safety, performance, and energy efficiency standards. These codes are designed to protect the health and safety of building occupants while also promoting energy conservation and environmental responsibility. HVAC standards are often developed by industry organizations and may cover everything from system design and installation to ongoing maintenance and inspection. It is important for homeowners and contractors to follow these codes and standards to avoid costly mistakes, ensure legal compliance, and optimize the system's performance. Following these guidelines also helps in avoiding issues such as poor air quality, inefficient energy use, and unsafe operating conditions.

ASHRAE and Other Industry Standards

ASHRAE (the American Society of Heating, Refrigerating, and Air-Conditioning Engineers) is one of the leading organizations that set industry standards for HVAC systems. ASHRAE's standards and guidelines are widely respected and help ensure that HVAC systems are designed, installed, and maintained to deliver high performance, comfort, and safety while also promoting energy efficiency and sustainability.

ASHRAE's standards cover various aspects of HVAC systems, including system design, ventilation, air quality, and energy efficiency. One of its most well-known standards is ASHRAE Standard 62.1, which focuses on ventilation for acceptable indoor air quality. This standard provides guidelines on how to ensure sufficient airflow and filtration to maintain healthy indoor air in buildings, which is essential for the well-being of the occupants. ASHRAE also offers standards related to energy efficiency, such as Standard 90.1, which outlines minimum energy performance requirements for HVAC systems in commercial buildings.

In addition to ASHRAE, there are other industry standards and codes that help guide HVAC system installation and maintenance. The International Mechanical Code (IMC) is another widely recognized set of guidelines that governs the installation and inspection of HVAC systems in buildings. The IMC covers aspects such as system design, safety, ventilation, and air distribution, ensuring that HVAC systems meet safety and performance standards.

The National Fire Protection Association (NFPA) also provides standards, particularly related to fire safety and prevention in HVAC systems. For example, NFPA 90A addresses the installation of air-conditioning and ventilation systems to prevent the spread of fire and smoke through ducts.

The Energy Star program, run by the U.S. Environmental Protection Agency (EPA), provides guidelines and certifications for energy-efficient HVAC systems. Products that meet Energy Star criteria are proven to be more energy-efficient, helping reduce energy consumption and lowering utility costs.

Compliance with these industry standards and codes is essential for homeowners, builders, and HVAC professionals. By following ASHRAE and other relevant standards, HVAC systems can be designed and installed to meet safety, performance, and energy efficiency requirements. This ensures the system operates optimally, reduces environmental impact, and keeps the indoor environment comfortable and healthy for its occupants.

16.2 HVAC and Fire Safety Considerations

Fire safety is a critical aspect of HVAC systems because they play a significant role in maintaining safe air circulation, especially in buildings where heating or cooling systems are involved. HVAC systems, particularly those involving combustion or ventilation, can pose fire risks if not properly designed, installed, and maintained. To ensure that HVAC systems do not contribute to fire hazards, it is essential to follow proper fire safety guidelines and regulations.

One of the key fire safety considerations in HVAC systems is the proper installation of components, such as gas furnaces or boilers, which involve combustion. These systems need to be properly vented to prevent the buildup of dangerous gases like carbon monoxide. When combustion gases are not vented correctly, they can accumulate in the building, leading to potential poisoning or fires. Ventilation ducts must be installed with clear and unobstructed paths to direct these gases outside.

Air ducts are another important component to consider for fire safety. Ducts should be made from materials that are fire-resistant and should be properly sealed to prevent the spread of smoke and flames in the event of a fire. Ducts should also be regularly inspected to ensure that there are no leaks or blockages that could hinder airflow or worsen a fire emergency. In addition, fire dampers can be installed in ducts to prevent fire from spreading through the ventilation system, which is especially important in large commercial buildings.

Filters and air vents should also be carefully maintained to avoid the buildup of dust and debris, which can be flammable. Regular cleaning of filters helps reduce the risk of dust catching fire, especially in older systems where dust can accumulate more easily. This is an important safety measure for both residential and commercial HVAC systems.

Another consideration for fire safety is the electrical system within the HVAC unit. HVAC systems rely heavily on electricity to power fans, compressors, and other components. If the system has faulty wiring or an electrical short, it can lead to overheating and increase the risk of fires. Regular inspections of the electrical components and ensuring that the wiring is up to code can help prevent such hazards.

Smoke and carbon monoxide detectors should also be installed in homes and buildings with HVAC systems. These detectors can alert residents to dangerous levels of smoke or carbon monoxide that may be present due to a malfunctioning HVAC system. It is important to test these detectors regularly to ensure they are working correctly and replace batteries as needed.

In addition to proper installation and maintenance, HVAC systems should be equipped with automatic shutoff mechanisms that turn the system off in the event of a fire or when dangerous conditions are detected. This feature can help minimize the spread of fire and reduce damage to the system and the building.

In conclusion, ensuring fire safety in HVAC systems involves careful planning, regular maintenance, and adherence to safety codes. Proper venting, the use of fire-resistant materials, regular cleaning of ducts and filters, and proper electrical inspections are essential to reducing the risk of fire hazards. By taking these precautions, homeowners and building managers can keep HVAC systems operating safely while reducing the potential for fires.

Part 9: Emerging Trends

Chapter Seventeen: Smart HVAC Systems and IOT Integration

Smart HVAC systems are the next step in the evolution of heating, ventilation, and air conditioning technology. These systems use advanced technology to improve efficiency, comfort, and control. The key feature of a smart HVAC system is its ability to connect to the Internet of Things, which allows users to control and monitor their HVAC systems remotely using smart phones, tablets, or computers.

One of the main benefits of smart HVAC systems is energy efficiency. With IOT integration, these systems can be programmed to adjust settings based on factors such as time of day, occupancy, and outside weather conditions. For example, the system can automatically lower the temperature when the house is empty and raise it again before you arrive home. This helps to save energy by reducing the amount of heating or cooling required when it is not needed, leading to lower utility bills.

Smart HVAC systems also provide better control and comfort. Through apps and smart home integration, users can adjust the temperature, humidity, and airflow settings without having to be physically present in the building. This remote control capability makes it easier to ensure that your home or office is always at a comfortable temperature, no matter where you are. Additionally, some smart HVAC systems can learn your preferences over time and adjust settings accordingly, offering a personalized experience.

IOT integration allows smart HVAC systems to be more responsive to changing conditions. For example, sensors can monitor indoor air quality, humidity, and temperature, providing real-time data. If any issue is detected, such as a sudden temperature spike or a decrease in air quality, the system can alert the user through a smart phone notification or even make automatic adjustments to correct the issue. This helps prevent problems before they become more serious, such as overheating or poor air quality.

Maintenance is another area where smart HVAC systems shine. These systems can track performance and usage data, making it easier to identify when maintenance or repairs are needed. For instance, if a filter needs to be replaced or a component is not working as efficiently as it should, the system can notify the homeowner or HVAC professional. This predictive maintenance helps avoid unexpected breakdowns and extends the lifespan of the system.

In conclusion, smart HVAC systems with IT integration provide convenience, comfort, and efficiency. By allowing remote control, offering real-time data monitoring, and enabling predictive maintenance, these systems can improve the overall experience of managing your home's heating and cooling needs. As technology continues to advance, smart HVAC systems will become even more sophisticated, making it easier for homeowners to manage energy use, enhance comfort, and save on energy costs.

17.1 Advances in HVAC Technology

Advances in HVAC technology have made systems more efficient, sustainable, and user-friendly. Over the years, innovations have led to smarter and more eco-friendly systems that not only provide better comfort but also help reduce energy consumption. Modern HVAC systems are equipped with features like variable-speed motors, advanced sensors, and smart thermostats, all of which improve performance and save energy. The use of renewable energy sources like solar power and geothermal energy is also becoming more common in HVAC systems, offering cleaner alternatives to traditional energy sources. Additionally, the integration of IOT (Internet of Things) technology allows users to remotely monitor and control their systems for greater convenience and efficiency. With these advancements, HVAC systems can now operate more efficiently, require less maintenance, and have a smaller environmental impact, helping both homeowners and businesses save money while supporting sustainability efforts.

1. Variable Refrigerant Flow (VRF) Systems

Variable Refrigerant Flow (VRF) systems are an advanced HVAC technology designed to provide efficient heating and cooling by controlling the flow of refrigerant to multiple indoor units. These systems are also known as Variable Refrigerant Volume (VRV) systems, a term coined by the company Daikin, which first introduced the technology. VRF systems are becoming increasingly popular in both commercial and residential buildings due to their flexibility, energy efficiency, and ability to control temperature independently in different zones.

At the heart of a VRF system is a central outdoor unit that is connected to multiple indoor units spread throughout the building. Unlike traditional HVAC systems that use a single duct or central unit for air distribution, VRF systems can control the refrigerant flow to each indoor unit based on the specific heating or cooling needs of each area. This allows for precise temperature control in different zones, making VRF systems ideal for buildings with varying space sizes, multiple rooms, or areas with different usage patterns.

One of the main benefits of VRF systems is their energy efficiency. Traditional HVAC systems operate at a fixed capacity, meaning they can waste energy by running at full power even when only partial cooling or heating is needed. In contrast, VRF systems use an inverter-driven compressor, which can adjust the speed of the compressor to match the demand for cooling or heating. This means that VRF systems only use the amount of energy required for the specific conditions, reducing energy waste and lowering utility costs.

Additionally, VRF systems offer the ability to simultaneously heat and cool different areas of a building. For example, while one room or zone is being cooled, another can be heated at the same time, which is particularly beneficial in larger spaces with different temperature needs. This feature is made possible by the advanced refrigerant management technology in the VRF system, allowing it to operate with high flexibility and responsiveness to varying temperature conditions.

Another advantage of VRF systems is their quiet operation. Since the system uses a variable-speed compressor and a decentralized setup with individual indoor units, it operates more quietly than traditional HVAC systems, which often rely on large, noisy fans and ducts. The indoor units are also smaller and more compact, making them less intrusive and easier to install in tight spaces.

VRF systems are also known for their ease of installation and versatility. Because they do not require large ductwork, they are well-suited for buildings where space for ducts is limited, or where aesthetic considerations require a less bulky HVAC setup. The systems can be installed in both new buildings and existing ones, making them a great choice for retrofits or renovations.

In conclusion, Variable Refrigerant Flow (VRF) systems represent a significant advancement in HVAC technology. They offer energy-efficient, flexible, and quiet solutions for heating and cooling in buildings of all sizes. With the ability to provide precise temperature control in multiple zones, VRF systems are ideal for both commercial and residential applications. They are helping to reduce energy consumption and improve comfort levels in modern buildings, making them an increasingly popular choice for sustainable and efficient HVAC solutions.

2. Advanced Air Purification Systems

Advanced air purification systems are an important innovation in HVAC technology, designed to improve indoor air quality by removing harmful particles, pollutants, and allergens from the air. These systems are especially useful in homes and commercial buildings where air quality can be affected by dust, pet dander, mold, smoke, chemicals, and other contaminants. With increasing awareness of health issues related to poor indoor air quality, advanced air purification systems have become a key feature in modern HVAC systems.

One of the most common types of advanced air purification systems is the HEPA (High-Efficiency Particulate Air) filter. HEPA filters can trap tiny particles as small as 0.3 microns, which includes dust, pollen, pet dander, and even some bacteria and viruses. These filters are highly effective at cleaning the air and are often used in conjunction with other filtration technologies to provide even cleaner air.

In addition to HEPA filters, many advanced air purification systems use activated carbon filters. Activated carbon is a highly porous material that can absorb odors, volatile organic compounds (VOCs), and gases such as smoke and cooking smells. This is especially helpful in environments where air pollutants like chemicals from cleaning products, paints, or industrial processes are present.

Another key technology in advanced air purification is ultraviolet (UV) light. UV germicidal lamps are installed in HVAC systems to kill bacteria, viruses, and mold spores. These systems work by emitting UV light that damages the DNA or RNA of microorganisms, rendering them harmless and preventing their spread. This type of air purification is often used in hospitals, offices, and homes where air quality and health are a top priority.

Ionization is another method used in advanced air purification. Ionizers release negatively charged ions into the air, which attach to positively charged particles such as dust, pollen, and smoke. Once the particles become heavy, they fall to the ground or get trapped in the air purifier's filters. This helps reduce the number of airborne contaminants and improve overall air quality.

Some advanced air purification systems also integrate multiple technologies to maximize their effectiveness. For example, a system might use a combination of HEPA filtration, activated carbon, and UV light to address a wide range of contaminants. These multi-stage systems are particularly effective in environments with high levels of pollutants, such as homes with smokers, pet owners, or areas with high levels of outdoor pollution.

The growing trend of "smart" air purifiers has also made its way into HVAC systems. These smart devices use sensors to monitor the air quality in real-time and adjust their operation accordingly. For example, if the system detects high levels of allergens or pollutants, it can automatically increase the filtration speed to clean the air more efficiently. Many smart air purifiers can be connected to mobile apps, allowing users to monitor and control the air quality remotely.

One of the main benefits of advanced air purification systems is the improvement of indoor air quality, which can help reduce the symptoms of allergies, asthma, and other respiratory issues. By removing harmful particles and pollutants from the air, these systems can create a healthier and more comfortable living or working environment.

In conclusion, advanced air purification systems are a key advancement in HVAC technology, designed to enhance indoor air quality and create healthier indoor environments. By utilizing a range of technologies such as HEPA filters, activated carbon, UV light, and ionization, these systems effectively remove airborne pollutants and allergens. As awareness of the importance of indoor air quality continues to grow, advanced air purification systems are becoming an essential part of modern HVAC systems in both residential and commercial settings.

17.2 The Future of HVAC: De-carbonization and Sustainability

The future of HVAC (Heating, Ventilation, and Air Conditioning) is moving toward de-carbonization and sustainability as the world becomes more focused on reducing its environmental impact. De-carbonization refers to the process of reducing carbon emissions, especially carbon dioxide (CO_2), which are a major contributor to climate change. The HVAC industry, which is responsible for a significant portion of global energy consumption and greenhouse gas emissions, is making major strides toward becoming more sustainable. These changes are driven by the need for cleaner energy, improved energy efficiency, and the reduction of harmful emissions.

One of the key aspects of de-carbonizing HVAC systems is shifting away from fossil fuels like natural gas and oil, which are commonly used in traditional heating systems. Many modern HVAC technologies are now designed to run on electricity, which can be sourced from renewable energy sources like solar, wind, and hydroelectric power. This shift is helping reduce the carbon footprint of HVAC systems. For example, heat pumps, which are an energy-efficient alternative to traditional heating and cooling systems, can be powered by electricity from renewable sources. By using less energy and relying on cleaner electricity, these systems help lower overall carbon emissions.

Another important development in the future of HVAC is the integration of renewable energy sources. Solar-powered HVAC systems, for instance, use solar panels to generate electricity, which can then be used to power heating and cooling equipment. This reduces the need for electricity from the grid, which often comes from non-renewable sources like coal or natural gas. In addition, geothermal heating and cooling systems use the earth's natural heat to provide temperature regulation, offering a sustainable alternative to traditional systems.

Energy efficiency plays a huge role in the future of HVAC systems. As buildings and homes become more energy-efficient, the demand for heating and cooling will decrease, which means that HVAC systems will use less energy. Technologies like variable refrigerant flow (VRF) systems, smart thermostats, and advanced sensors allow HVAC systems to adjust their operation based on real-time conditions, ensuring that energy is used only when necessary. This leads to significant reductions in energy waste, and less energy use means fewer emissions.

In addition to improving the energy efficiency of HVAC systems, there is also a focus on using refrigerants that are less harmful to the environment. Many traditional refrigerants, such as hydro-fluorocarbons (HFCs), have a high global warming potential (GWP), meaning they contribute significantly to climate change if released into the atmosphere. Newer, more environmentally friendly refrigerants are being developed and adopted to replace these harmful substances. For example, refrigerants with a lower GWP are being used in many modern systems, helping to reduce the environmental impact of HVAC systems.

Sustainability also extends to the materials used in HVAC systems. Manufacturers are increasingly using recyclable, non-toxic, and environmentally friendly materials to build HVAC components. This not only reduces the carbon footprint of manufacturing HVAC systems but also ensures that the systems themselves can be more easily recycled or repurposed at the end of their life cycle.

Smart HVAC technology is another crucial part of the future. With advancements in IoT (Internet of Things) and smart home devices, HVAC systems can now be controlled and monitored remotely. Smart thermostats and sensors can optimize energy use by learning the behavior of the occupants and adjusting the temperature accordingly. This kind of smart system helps reduce unnecessary heating or cooling and ensures that energy is used efficiently. Additionally, data collected from these systems can be analyzed to identify areas for improvement and optimize performance over time.

Finally, the future of HVAC will likely involve stronger collaboration between the HVAC industry and the renewable energy sector. By working together, these industries can create more integrated solutions that combine energy-efficient HVAC systems with solar, wind, or other renewable energy sources, making homes and buildings more self-sufficient and environmentally friendly.

In conclusion, the future of HVAC is focused on de-carbonization, sustainability, and energy efficiency. As the world continues to address climate change, HVAC systems are evolving to reduce carbon emissions, increase energy efficiency, and integrate renewable energy sources. These advancements are helping to create a more sustainable future, where HVAC systems play a crucial role in reducing environmental impact while maintaining comfort and functionality in buildings and homes.

Part 10: HVAC for Specific Applications

Chapter Eighteen: Residential HVAC Systems

Residential HVAC systems are essential for keeping homes comfortable throughout the year by controlling temperature, humidity, and air quality. HVAC stands for Heating, Ventilation, and Air Conditioning, and these systems combine all three functions to create a pleasant indoor environment. Whether it is heating your home in the winter, cooling it in the summer, or ensuring good air quality year-round, residential HVAC systems make living spaces more comfortable and healthier.

1. Heating: In colder months, the heating component of the HVAC system keeps the home warm. The most common types of heating systems in residential HVAC include furnaces, boilers, and heat pumps. Furnaces heat air and distribute it through the home via ducts, while boilers heat water to provide hot water or steam for radiators. Heat pumps, on the other hand, can both heat and cool a home by transferring heat between the house and the outside air or ground.

2. Air Conditioning: During hot weather, air conditioning cools the home. Central air conditioning is a common system that uses a network of ducts to distribute cool air throughout the house. Other options include window units, which are ideal for cooling individual rooms, and mini-split systems, which are ductless and provide cooling for specific areas. All these systems work by using refrigerants to absorb heat from inside the house and release it outside.

3. Ventilation: Proper ventilation is necessary for good air quality and comfort. Ventilation helps remove stale air and introduces fresh air into the home. This can be done through natural ventilation, like opening windows, or mechanical systems such as exhaust fans and air exchange systems that continuously bring in fresh air while removing pollutants. Balanced ventilation systems, like heat recovery ventilators (HRV) and energy recovery ventilators (ERV), are designed to improve both indoor air quality and energy efficiency by exchanging indoor air with fresh outdoor air while minimizing heat loss.

4. Air Filtration and Purification: Air filters are an important part of any residential HVAC system, as they help remove dust, dirt, pollen, and other particles from the air. Many modern systems come with high-efficiency filters that can capture very small particles, improving air quality and reducing allergens. In addition to basic filtration, some systems also have air purifiers that help eliminate odors, bacteria, viruses, and other contaminants in the air.

5. Control Systems (Thermostats): The thermostat is the control center for a residential HVAC system. It allows homeowners to set the desired temperature for heating or cooling. Modern thermostats are often "smart," meaning they can be controlled remotely via a smart phone app and can learn the homeowner's preferences to adjust the temperature automatically. Smart thermostats can help improve energy efficiency by adjusting the temperature based on whether the home is occupied or not.

Types of Residential HVAC Systems

There are several types of HVAC systems that homeowners can choose from, depending on the size of the home, the local climate, and the homeowner's needs:

a. Central HVAC Systems: These systems provide heating and cooling to an entire home through a series of ducts. A central unit, such as a furnace or air handler, is connected to ducts that distribute air to each room. Central HVAC systems are ideal for larger homes or homes with multiple rooms.

b. Ductless Systems: For homes that don't have existing ductwork, ductless systems like mini-split systems are an option. These systems provide both heating and cooling, and they are typically installed with an outdoor unit and one or more indoor air handlers mounted on walls. Ductless systems are more energy-efficient and offer flexibility in controlling the temperature in individual rooms.

c. Window and Portable Units: For smaller homes or individual rooms, window air conditioners and portable units are cost-effective solutions. These units are easy to install and can be moved from room to room, but they do not provide whole-home heating or cooling.

Benefits of Residential HVAC Systems

a. Comfort: Residential HVAC systems are designed to maintain a comfortable temperature and humidity level inside the home. Whether it is winter or summer, these systems keep the home environment at a comfortable level for all family members.

b. Energy Efficiency: Modern residential HVAC systems are more energy-efficient than ever. High-efficiency furnaces, air conditioners, and heat pumps use less energy to perform the same tasks, helping homeowners save on energy bills. Properly sized and well-maintained systems can also run more efficiently, further reducing energy consumption.

c. Improved Indoor Air Quality: Many HVAC systems come with air filtration and purification features, which help improve indoor air quality by removing allergens, dust, and pollutants. This is particularly beneficial for people with allergies or respiratory issues.

d. Convenience and Control: With advancements in technology, residential HVAC systems offer greater control over your home's climate. Smart thermostats and mobile apps allow homeowners to adjust settings from anywhere, ensuring the home is always at the ideal temperature.

Maintaining Your Residential HVAC System

To ensure that your residential HVAC system works efficiently, regular maintenance is important. This includes cleaning or replacing air filters, checking for leaks in ducts, ensuring proper airflow, and scheduling professional inspections for system components such as the furnace, air conditioner, and heat pump. Proper maintenance helps extend the lifespan of the system, prevent costly repairs, and keep energy costs down.

In conclusion, residential HVAC systems are vital for maintaining comfort, improving air quality, and ensuring energy efficiency in homes. Whether you are looking for a system to heat or cool your space, or you want to improve indoor air quality, HVAC systems offer various options to meet your needs. By choosing the right system and maintaining it properly, you can create a more comfortable and energy-efficient home environment.

18.1 Commercial and Industrial HVAC Systems

Commercial and industrial HVAC systems are designed to provide heating, cooling, ventilation, and air quality control in large buildings, factories, offices, retail spaces, and other commercial or industrial facilities. These systems are generally larger, more complex, and more powerful than residential HVAC systems, as they are built to handle the greater demands of a larger space or specific industrial processes. They are critical in maintaining a comfortable, safe, and healthy environment for workers, customers, and visitors in these types of spaces.

1. Heating and Cooling Needs: Commercial and industrial HVAC systems need to provide both heating and cooling across large spaces with varying demands. These systems must be able to maintain consistent temperatures in areas with a lot of people, machinery, or specialized equipment. For example, offices may require cooling during the summer, while a factory may need heating during the winter to maintain optimal working conditions.

The most common types of heating and cooling systems used in commercial and industrial buildings are:

a. Centralized Air Conditioning Systems: Large air handlers and chillers are used to cool the air in the building, and ductwork distributes the cool air throughout the space.

b. Unitary HVAC Systems: These systems are often used for smaller commercial buildings or zones. They include packaged units that combine the heating and cooling functions into a single system.

c. Heat Pumps: In some commercial and industrial applications, heat pumps can provide both heating and cooling by transferring heat between indoor and outdoor environments.

2. Ventilation and Air Quality: Good ventilation is critical in commercial and industrial HVAC systems to ensure the health and comfort of building occupants. Proper ventilation also helps manage humidity levels and remove contaminants from the air, such as dust, fumes, and chemicals, which can be present in industrial settings.

a. Make-up Air Systems: These systems provide fresh air to replace the air that is exhausted from the building, ensuring that the indoor air quality remains optimal.

b. Exhaust Ventilation: For industrial facilities, it is important to remove harmful gases, fumes, or pollutants generated by manufacturing processes. Exhaust systems are used to pull contaminated air from work areas and expel it outside.

c. Air Filtration Systems: Commercial HVAC systems often include advanced filters to remove pollutants, allergens, and particulate matter from the air, improving indoor air quality. High-efficiency particulate air (HEPA) filters or other specialized filters may be used in places where air quality is of utmost importance.

3. Types of Commercial and Industrial HVAC Systems: Commercial and industrial HVAC systems vary depending on the size, function, and complexity of the building or facility. Some common types include:

a. Chilled Beam Systems: Used in commercial buildings, these systems use water-cooled beams to absorb heat from the air and provide cooling.

b. Variable Air Volume (VAV) Systems: These systems are used in larger commercial buildings to adjust the flow of air according to the specific heating or cooling requirements of different zones in the building. VAV systems are efficient because they only use as much air as needed to maintain the desired temperature.

c. Packaged Rooftop Units (RTUs): Many commercial buildings use packaged rooftop units that provide both heating and cooling. These units are located on the roof to save indoor space and are common in retail stores, office buildings, and schools.

d. Geothermal HVAC Systems: In certain industrial applications, geothermal systems use the earth's natural temperature to heat or cool a building. These systems are energy-efficient but require significant upfront investment.

4. Energy Efficiency: Energy efficiency is a key consideration in commercial and industrial HVAC systems. These systems often need to operate for extended hours, sometimes 24/7, which can lead to high energy costs if not managed correctly. Implementing energy-efficient HVAC systems helps reduce operating costs and meet sustainability goals.

a. Variable Refrigerant Flow (VRF) Systems: VRF systems are becoming more popular in commercial applications because they can adjust refrigerant flow to different zones depending on the cooling and heating requirements. This makes them highly efficient, as energy is only used when and where it's needed.

b. Smart Controls and Building Management Systems: Many commercial HVAC systems now incorporate smart controls and building management systems (BMS) that use sensors and data analytics to optimize energy use. These systems can monitor temperature, humidity, and air quality in real-time and adjust HVAC operations for maximum efficiency.

5. Specialized HVAC Systems for Industrial Applications: In industrial environments, HVAC systems must often meet very specific needs, such as controlling temperature and humidity for sensitive equipment or maintaining air purity for manufacturing processes. Some specialized systems include:

a. Clean Room HVAC Systems: Used in industries like pharmaceuticals or electronics, clean room systems must filter and control air quality to very strict standards. They maintain a controlled environment by filtering air to remove particles, controlling humidity, and maintaining temperature consistency.

b. Industrial Refrigeration Systems: These systems are used in industries like food processing, warehouses, and cold storage, where maintaining a low temperature is critical. Industrial refrigeration systems can cool large spaces or keep products at the desired temperature.

c. Process Cooling Systems: These systems are designed to cool machinery or industrial processes that generate a lot of heat, such as in data centers, factories, or chemical plants. They help ensure that equipment operates at optimal temperatures, reducing the risk of overheating and damage.

6. Maintenance and Monitoring: Commercial and industrial HVAC systems require regular maintenance to ensure they continue to operate effectively. Routine checks for airflow, filter replacements, and system inspections are essential to keep systems running smoothly. Preventative maintenance can help avoid costly repairs and downtime.

In addition to regular maintenance, many HVAC systems in commercial and industrial settings are now equipped with advanced monitoring tools that allow facility managers to track performance remotely. These systems alert the staff to potential problems, such as equipment malfunctions or drops in efficiency, before they cause significant issues.

Conclusion: Commercial and industrial HVAC systems are complex, large-scale systems designed to provide heating, cooling, and ventilation for various building types and industrial operations. These systems need to be energy-efficient, capable of handling large demands, and flexible enough to meet the specific needs of businesses and industries. Whether it is keeping a large office building comfortable, controlling air quality in a manufacturing facility, or maintaining optimal temperatures in a warehouse, commercial and industrial HVAC systems are vital to creating safe, comfortable, and efficient environments.

18.2 HVAC in Specialized Environments

HVAC systems in specialized environments are designed to meet the unique needs of specific spaces where temperature, humidity, air quality, and other conditions must be tightly controlled. These environments often require more advanced or tailored HVAC solutions than standard systems used in homes or offices. For example, hospitals need HVAC systems that can maintain clean, sterile air to protect patients from infections, while data centers need systems to keep sensitive electronics cool and prevent overheating. In industries like pharmaceuticals or food processing, temperature and humidity levels must be controlled precisely to ensure product quality and safety. HVAC systems in these settings are often equipped with specialized filters, sensors, and monitoring systems to meet strict regulations and maintain the desired conditions.

1. In hospitals and laboratories, HVAC systems play a critical role in maintaining a safe, healthy, and comfortable environment for patients, medical staff, and researchers. These environments

require specialized HVAC systems because they have unique needs when it comes to air quality, temperature, and humidity control.

In hospitals, the HVAC system must help create conditions that promote patient recovery while also ensuring the safety and comfort of medical staff. The system needs to maintain specific temperatures in different areas of the hospital, such as operating rooms, patient rooms, and waiting areas. Operating rooms, for example, need to be kept at a lower temperature to control bacteria growth and maintain sterile conditions. Additionally, they require positive pressure to prevent contamination from entering the room. In contrast, patient rooms may need to be kept at a comfortable temperature for patients while also ensuring proper air circulation.

Hospitals also require a high level of air filtration. HVAC systems are often equipped with HEPA (High-Efficiency Particulate Air) filters that trap small particles, bacteria, and viruses, reducing the risk of infection. Clean, filtered air is crucial for patient recovery, especially for those with weakened immune systems, such as those undergoing surgery or chemotherapy.

In laboratories, HVAC systems are designed to protect both the people working in the space and the experiments or products being handled. Laboratories often require strict control over temperature and humidity to prevent contamination or degradation of sensitive materials. For example, pharmaceutical labs may need to maintain precise temperatures to ensure the stability of chemicals, vaccines, or other substances being researched or developed.

In these specialized environments, the HVAC system must also maintain a constant airflow to ensure proper ventilation and remove hazardous fumes or chemicals. Laboratories that deal with dangerous substances, like biological agents or toxic chemicals, require more advanced systems with specialized filtration (such as chemical scrubbers or fume hoods) to safely handle and remove contaminants from the air.

In both hospitals and laboratories, the HVAC system must be designed to meet local and national codes and regulations. These codes set standards for air quality, temperature, and humidity, ensuring that the systems protect health and safety. Given the importance of these systems in such environments, regular maintenance and monitoring are crucial to ensure everything is functioning properly.

In conclusion, HVAC systems in hospitals and laboratories are more complex than typical systems because they must provide safe, clean, and comfortable conditions. These systems need to manage temperature, humidity, and airflow precisely, while also filtering out contaminants and maintaining air quality. Properly designed and maintained HVAC systems in these specialized environments are essential for the health, safety, and success of medical and scientific work.

2. Data centers: Data centers are specialized environments where HVAC systems play a crucial role in keeping the technology and equipment running smoothly. These centers house large numbers of servers, computers, and other electronic devices that store, process, and manage data.

Since these devices generate a lot of heat, the HVAC system in data centers must be carefully designed to prevent overheating, which can cause equipment failure or system downtime.

The primary function of HVAC in data centers is to regulate temperature and humidity levels to ensure that the equipment operates within safe limits. Servers and other electronic components generate a significant amount of heat during operation, so the HVAC system must effectively remove this heat to maintain a cool environment. If the temperature gets too high, it can damage sensitive equipment, leading to costly repairs or loss of data. Therefore, data centers often need to maintain a steady temperature, typically between 68°F to 72°F (20°C to 22°C), with humidity levels kept between 45% to 55%.

To manage the heat load, data centers typically use high-efficiency cooling systems such as Computer Room Air Conditioning (CRAC) units or Computer Room Air Handler (CRAH) systems. These units work to cool the air and maintain a consistent temperature throughout the space. Some data centers also use raised floors to distribute cool air more evenly or cold aisle and hot aisle configurations to optimize airflow.

In addition to cooling, data centers require efficient airflow management. The HVAC system must ensure that cool air is directed towards the servers, while warm air is removed effectively. This involves the use of ducts, fans, and airflow containment strategies to ensure that hot and cold air do not mix, as mixing can reduce the effectiveness of cooling efforts.

Moreover, HVAC systems in data centers must be highly reliable. Data centers often operate 24/7 and cannot afford system failures that could lead to downtime or loss of service. This means that HVAC systems need to be equipped with backup power sources, such as generators or uninterruptible power supplies (UPS), to ensure continued operation in the event of power loss.

Energy efficiency is also a significant consideration in data center HVAC systems. Since cooling systems can consume large amounts of energy, many data centers aim to reduce their energy consumption by implementing energy-saving technologies. This may include using advanced cooling techniques like free cooling (which uses outside air for cooling when the weather allows) or liquid cooling for specific equipment. Monitoring and optimizing the HVAC system for energy efficiency is essential to reduce operating costs and minimize the environmental impac, HVAC systems in data centers are vital for maintaining the right conditions for sensitive equipment to function properly. These systems need to manage temperature, humidity, and airflow carefully, using advanced cooling technologies and energy-efficient solutions to ensure the data center operates efficiently and without interruption. Properly designed HVAC systems are crucial for the reliability, performance, and longevity of the equipment housed in data centers.

3. In greenhouses, HVAC systems are essential for creating and maintaining the ideal environment for plant growth. Unlike typical buildings, greenhouses require careful control of temperature, humidity, airflow, and light, as these factors directly affect the health and

productivity of plants. HVAC systems in greenhouses must ensure that the plants receive the right conditions throughout the year, whether it is hot summer days or cold winter nights.

The primary function of HVAC in a greenhouse is to regulate temperature and humidity levels. Different plants have specific requirements for these conditions, so the system must be flexible and capable of adjusting to the needs of various crops. For example, some plants thrive in warm, humid environments, while others may need cooler, drier conditions. Therefore, greenhouse HVAC systems must have the ability to maintain a stable temperature range, typically between 65°F and 75°F (18°C to 24°C), and manage humidity levels to avoid excess moisture, which can lead to mold or mildew growth.

To maintain the desired temperature, greenhouse HVAC systems often use a combination of heating, cooling, and ventilation. During colder months, heating systems such as gas, electric, or hydronic heaters help maintain warmth for the plants. In contrast, during hot summer days, cooling systems, like fans, evaporative coolers, or even air conditioning units, may be used to prevent overheating and ensure that the greenhouse remains at a comfortable temperature for plant growth.

Ventilation is also a key component of greenhouse HVAC systems. Proper airflow is necessary to prevent the buildup of stagnant air and ensure that plants receive fresh oxygen. Natural ventilation can be used by opening windows or vents to let cool air in and hot air out. However, in larger greenhouses or when external temperatures are not ideal, mechanical ventilation may be required. Exhaust fans and intake fans work together to create a constant flow of fresh air, helping to regulate the temperature and reduce humidity to the desired level.

In addition to temperature and humidity control, HVAC systems in greenhouses also often include air filtration. This ensures that the air inside the greenhouse remains free from pollutants, pests, and other contaminants that could harm plants. Filters can trap dust, dirt, and other particles, preventing them from entering the growing area.

In modern greenhouses, energy efficiency is becoming more important, and many systems are being designed to minimize energy consumption while maintaining optimal growing conditions. Some greenhouses use advanced technologies like smart thermostats and environmental sensors to monitor temperature, humidity, and light levels continuously. These systems can adjust the HVAC settings automatically based on real-time conditions, reducing energy waste.

In conclusion, HVAC systems in greenhouses are crucial for providing the right environment for plant growth. They regulate temperature, humidity, and airflow to ensure that plants thrive, whether it is hot or cold outside. With the use of advanced technologies and efficient energy management, greenhouse HVAC systems can help ensure healthy plants and sustainable growing practices.

Conclusion

Your Next Steps in HVAC: From Learning to Doing

Now that you have gained a solid understanding of HVAC basics, you might be wondering, What is next; Learning about HVAC is just the beginning, real progress comes when you put that knowledge into action. Whether you want to improve your home's HVAC system, start a career in the industry, or simply expand your skills, here are the next steps to take.

1. Apply What You have Learned

The best way to reinforce your knowledge is through hands-on experience. Here is how you can start:

a. Observe Your Own HVAC System: Take a closer look at your home's heating and cooling system. Identify its main components, check how the thermostat works, and listen to how the system operates.

b. Perform Basic Maintenance: Try simple tasks like replacing air filters, cleaning vents, and adjusting thermostat settings for efficiency.

c. Monitor Performance: Pay attention to how your HVAC system runs. Does it heat or cool effectively? Do you notice unusual noises? Observing these things will improve your troubleshooting skills.

2. Continue Learning and Expanding Your Knowledge

HVAC is a broad field, and there is always more to learn. Here are some ways to deepen your understanding:

a. Read More HVAC Books and Articles: Keep building your knowledge by exploring books, blogs, and industry magazines.

b. Watch Online Tutorials: Many professionals share tips and demonstrations online that can help you visualize HVAC concepts in action.

c. Join HVAC Forums and Communities: Engaging with others who share your interest can give you new insights and help answer any questions you may have.

3. Gain Hands-On Experience

If you are interested in working in the HVAC industry or becoming more skilled, hands-on experience is key. Here is how you can start:

a. Take an HVAC Course: Many community colleges and technical schools offer beginner-friendly HVAC programs that provide practical training.

b. Find a Mentor: If you know an HVAC professional, ask if you can observe their work or assist with simple tasks. Learning from experienced technicians is invaluable.

c. Experiment with Small DIY Projects: Try installing a smart thermostat, sealing air leaks, or checking your ductwork for efficiency. These small projects can boost your confidence.

4. Consider a Career in HVAC

If you are thinking about a career in HVAC, here are some steps to take:

a. Look Into Certification Programs: Earning an HVAC certification (like EPA 608 for refrigerant handling) can open doors to job opportunities.

b. Apply for an Apprenticeship: Many companies offer apprentice programs where you can train while working.

c. Explore Job Opportunities: HVAC technicians, installers, and maintenance specialists are in high demand. Research job options that match your interests.

5. Stay Updated and Keep Practicing

The HVAC industry is always evolving, with new technologies and energy-efficient solutions emerging. Staying up to date will keep your skills sharp.

a. Follow Industry Trends: Learn about smart HVAC systems, energy-saving advancements, and eco-friendly solutions.

b. Continue Practicing: The more you work with HVAC systems, the more comfortable and skilled you'll become.

Whether your goal is to maintain your home's HVAC system, expand your skills, or start a career in the field, the most important step is to take action. Keep learning, get hands-on experience, and do not be afraid to ask questions.

Encouragement for Further Study and Professional Opportunities

The HVAC industry is constantly growing because heating, cooling, and ventilation are essential for homes, businesses, and industries. This means skilled professionals are always in demand. If you enjoy working with your hands, solving problems, and making people's homes or workplaces more comfortable, HVAC could be a great career choice.

If you are interested in further study, there are many ways to expand your knowledge.. Many community colleges and trade schools offer hands-on training programs that teach everything from system installation to troubleshooting. These courses can help you build confidence and prepare you for more advanced HVAC work.

For those considering a career in HVAC, certification is an important step. Many employers look for certified technicians who have completed training and passed industry-recognized exams. Certifications. Some HVAC technicians start by working as apprentices, learning from experienced professionals while earning a paycheck. Over time, you can gain the skills needed to become a full-time technician, supervisor, or even start your own HVAC business.

Beyond technical skills, HVAC also offers opportunities for specialization. Some professionals focus on energy-efficient systems, helping people save money and reduce their environmental impact. Others work on large commercial buildings, hospitals, or data centers, ensuring that critical equipment stays at the right temperature. If you enjoy technology, you can explore smart HVAC systems, which use automation and remote controls to improve energy use.

Even if you do not plan to work in HVAC professionally, further study can help you maintain your own system, save on repair costs, and make better decisions when upgrading or replacing equipment. Understanding HVAC allows you to improve energy efficiency in your home, improve indoor air quality, and troubleshoot minor issues before they become major problems.

No matter your goal whether it is gaining more knowledge, saving money, improving home comfort, or starting a rewarding career. The HVAC field offers endless opportunities to learn and grow. Keep exploring, stay curious, and never stop learning. The more you know the more valuable your skills will become.

Appendices

Glossary of HVAC Terms

Comprehensive List of HVAC Key Terms and Their Definitions

Understanding HVAC (Heating, Ventilation, and Air Conditioning) can be easier when you know the key terms used in the industry. Below is a comprehensive list of important HVAC terms and their simple definitions.

General HVAC Terms

HVAC – Stands for Heating, Ventilation, and Air Conditioning, which refers to systems that control indoor temperature, air quality, and airflow.

Thermal Comfort: The condition where people feel neither too hot nor too cold, but just right.

BTU (British Thermal Unit): A unit that measures heat energy. In HVAC, it tells how much heat a system can add or remove from the air.

Ton (Cooling Capacity): A measurement of an air conditioners cooling ability. One ton equals the cooling power of melting 2,000 pounds of ice in 24 hours.

CFM (Cubic Feet per Minute): Measures airflow. It tells how much air moves through a system in one minute.

Refrigeration Cycle: The process in which heat is removed from the air using refrigerant, cooling coils, and a compressor.

Heating Terms

Furnace: A heating system that generates heat by burning fuel (gas, oil) or using electricity.

Boiler: A heating device that uses water or steam to transfer heat through radiators or pipes.

Heat Pump: A system that moves heat from one place to another. It can heat a home in winter and cool it in summer.

Combustion Chamber: The part of a furnace where fuel is burned to create heat.

Pilot Light: A small flame that ignites the gas burner in older furnaces.

AFUE (Annual Fuel Utilization Efficiency): A percentage that shows how efficiently a furnace converts fuel into heat. A higher AFUE means better efficiency.

Cooling and Refrigeration Terms

Air Conditioner (AC): A system that removes heat from indoor air to cool a space.

Refrigerant: A special fluid that absorbs and releases heat to cool the air in an AC or heat pump.

Compressor: A key part of an AC or heat pump that increases refrigerant pressure to help it move heat.

Evaporator Coil: A coil inside the indoor unit that absorbs heat from the air, cooling it down.

Condenser Coil: A coil in the outdoor unit that releases the heat collected from indoors.

SEER (Seasonal Energy Efficiency Ratio): A rating that measures the efficiency of an air conditioner. Higher SEER means better energy savings.

Dehumidifier: A device that removes excess moisture from the air, improving comfort and air quality.

Ventilation and Airflow Terms

Ventilation: The process of bringing fresh air in and removing stale air from a building.

Ductwork: A system of tubes that distribute heated or cooled air throughout a building.

Return Air: Air that is pulled back into the HVAC system to be heated or cooled again.

Supply Air: The conditioned air that is sent into rooms through vents.

Air Filter: A filter that removes dust, allergens, and pollutants from the air before it enters the system.

ERV (Energy Recovery Ventilator): A system that improves ventilation while saving energy by transferring heat and moisture between incoming and outgoing air.

MERV Rating (Minimum Efficiency Reporting Value): A scale that measures how well an air filter traps particles. Higher numbers mean better filtration.

Thermostat and Control Terms

Thermostat: A device that controls the temperature by turning the HVAC system on or off as needed.

Smart Thermostat: A programmable thermostat that can learn your schedule and be controlled remotely through an app.

Set point: The temperature you set on your thermostat for heating or cooling.

Zoning System: A setup that allows different areas (zones) in a building to have different temperatures for better comfort and efficiency.

HVAC Load Calculation: A calculation used to determine the heating and cooling needs of a space based on size, insulation, and climate.

Energy Efficiency and Environmental Terms

Energy Star: A government-backed certification for appliances that meet high energy efficiency standards.

HSPF (Heating Seasonal Performance Factor): A rating that measures the efficiency of a heat pump in heating mode. Higher numbers mean better efficiency.

R-22 (Freon) and R-410A: Types of refrigerants used in AC systems, R-22 is being phased out due to environmental concerns, while R-410A is the newer, eco-friendly option.

Insulation: Material that helps keep heat inside during winter and outside during summer, reducing HVAC system workload.

Air Sealing: The process of closing leaks around doors, windows, and ducts to prevent heated or cooled air from escaping.

Maintenance and Repair Terms

HVAC Tune-Up: A routine maintenance check-up to keep the system running efficiently and prevent breakdowns.

Blower Motor: The motor that powers the fan, moving air through the ducts.

Coil Cleaning: The process of removing dust and dirt from evaporator and condenser coils to improve efficiency.

Refrigerant Leak: A problem where refrigerant escapes from the system, reducing cooling power and efficiency.

Short Cycling: When an HVAC system turns on and off too frequently, usually due to a malfunction or incorrect sizing.

System Pressure: The measure of pressure inside refrigerant lines, which helps diagnose HVAC performance.

Air Balancing: Adjusting airflow through ducts to ensure even heating or cooling in all rooms.

Learning these key HVAC terms will help you better understand how heating, cooling, and ventilation systems work. Whether you are a homeowner, a student, or considering an HVAC career, knowing these terms will make it easier to communicate with professionals, troubleshoot problems, and make informed decisions about your system.

By familiarizing yourself with this vocabulary, you're taking another important step on your HVAC journey.